D1565460

The Revolutionary Disciple draws from years of experience as well as countless hours of implementation to present a comprehensive discipleship strategy for your home, work, and church. You'll benefit greatly from reading this book with your discipleship group or church staff.

Robby Gallaty, pastor and author of *Replicate*

This book is a long overdue call to us as leaders to humble ourselves before the Lord and the people we lead. The Western Church is not exempt from the self-blinding sin of pride nor its disastrous consequences. We will not be able to take ground for the kingdom until we deal with arrogance. That is Jim Putman and Chad Harrington's objective in *The Revolutionary Disciple*.

Ed Litton, pastor and president of the
Southern Baptist Convention

This incisive book offers readers different perspectives on some of the most important areas impacting the lives of Christ-followers. It is provocative and well worth the read.

Carol M. Swain, PhD, editor of *Be the People News*

The Revolutionary Disciple has me in a state of anxious introspection: my role as a talk radio host, my belief that the hardcore Left has fallen under spiritual evil that requires us to perform a counterrevolution, and my cherished identity as a Jesus follower are in a state of collision. I continue to think we need a counterrevolution, and this book lays out the way to the only lasting one. *The Revolutionary Disciple* presents the ultimate revolution, which as it happens is also the solution for our conscience and the only hope for our souls: we must come to act with the outrageous, shocking, and brave humility of Jesus Christ in all the spheres our lives cover.

Todd Herman, regular guest host for
The Rush Limbaugh Show

Undivided hearts. We want to be authentic disciples who change the world by making more disciples, but our pride prevents us from fully submitting to Jesus' lordship. Harrington and Putman expertly blend story and Scripture with practical tips. The result: wisdom for how to develop single-minded loyalty to King Jesus.

Matthew W. Bates, author of *Gospel Allegiance* and associate professor of theology at Quincy University

Jim Putman has done it again, this time in partnership with Chad Harrington. Their five spheres framework provides a breakthrough construct to guide believers into being disciples. In a straightforward, vulnerable style Jim and Chad provide a roadmap to a better place than where many of us were heading. The secret sauce—humility. It is literally breathtaking how far Jesus' brand of humility will take us in all the spheres of our lives. Who doesn't want that? Warning—while you will most definitely enjoy this book, Jim and Chad are not quite satisfied with that outcome. They are going to call us to actually give it a try. It will require something from us, but it will result in a glorious ending.

Randy Frazee, pastor and author of *His Mighty Strength*

The Revolutionary Disciple makes a much-needed case for a discipleship path that fully integrates all of our relationships and every area of our lives. You'll find it a helpful antidote to the self-centered "it's all about me and Jesus" path that so many have taken.

Larry Osborne, author and teaching pastor at North Coast Church

The Revolutionary Disciple calls us to approach all aspects of life with humility and a revolutionary-spirit disciplined by God's love and Christ's relentless sacrifice. This book is a gift the post-pandemic church needs to embrace, a practical guide challenging us to set aside our pride and walk humbly in the footsteps of Jesus toward the church of tomorrow that longs not to be served but to serve.

Shane J. Wood, professor at Ozark Christian College and best-selling author of *Between Two Trees*

The authors issue both a warning and a guide to avoid spiritual pride and how it destroys our work and our souls. This is worth the read. They have peeled back the layers of human personality and motivation and exposed our immaterial natures. Please read it, pray through it, and then follow their advice.

Bill Hull, cofounder of The Bonhoeffer Project and author of *The Cost of Cheap Grace* and *The Discipleship Gospel*

Most Christians realize that the first step to becoming a genuine child of God is humility. What they tend to forget is that humility is also the ongoing posture required if they ever want to come close to being mature disciples of the same God who saved them. The benefits that come with being a serious disciple of Jesus are consistently blocked by our human pride. Jim Putman and Chad Harrington know all about the underbelly of pride and how it undermines so much of what we are and could become as followers of Christ. In their vital book *The Revolutionary Disciple*, they honestly and transparently take their own pride to the woodshed and in the process show all of us how to humbly put God and keep God in his rightful place in our lives—the driver's seat.

Dr. Tim Kimmel, author of *Grace-Based Parenting* and *Grace-Filled Marriage*

Great, substantive message in short, readable chapters. I would recommend it highly without knowing the authors, but because I do life closely with both and know how they live, I more than highly recommend it.

Bobby Harrington, pastor, author, and CEO of Discipleship.org and Renew.org

Nothing is more radical nor revolutionary than answering the call to follow Jesus as disciples. Here is a book that has timeless answers for being a disciple in today's world. I am happy to recommend to you *The Revolutionary Disciple* by Putman and Harrington.

Rev. Dr. Winfield Bevins, director of church planting at Asbury Seminary and author of *Marks of a Movement*

An easy-to-remember five-sphere model for humble discipleship supported by practical ways to develop humility in each sphere. Read this book if you believe Jesus' words that "those who humble themselves will be exalted." And then act like it.

Renée Webb Sproles, director of cultural engagement at Renew.org

Addressing a rarely mentioned subject, Jim and Chad tackle an absolutely critical aspect of successful discipling . . . humility. A challenging subject that demands some honest evaluation and thought by every disciple maker. An excellent resource to read, ponder, discuss, and allow God to use in our own lives. I highly recommend this book to you.

Dr. Dann Spader, author of *4 Chair Discipling* and founder of Sonlife and Concentricglobal.org

The

REVOLUTIONARY DISCIPLE

Nashville, Tennessee

To my mom, Bobbi, and my dad, Bill—a humble
couple who gave their all to the very end.

— Jim

To Nanny and Papa,
who learned to walk humbly with Christ
even with the odds against them.

— Chad

CONTENTS

Acknowledgements 11
Introduction: A Real Life Battle 13

1. Is It Time for Another Revolution? 25
2. Humble Discipleship 37
3. The Revolutionary Disciple 49
4. The Profile of a Revolutionary 59

Bridge: Walking Through the Five Spheres 69

SPHERE 1: ABIDING IN CHRIST

5. The Yoke of Christ 77
6. Abiding with Humility 85
7. Humble Listening 95

SPHERE 2: THE CHURCH SPHERE

8. It's God's Church, Not Ours 107
9. Embracing God's Church 117
10. Navigating Submission in the Church 127

SPHERE 3: THE HOME SPHERE

11. When Church Becomes Family 137
12. Revolutionary Families 147
13. Walking Humbly with Your Spouse 155
14. Humble Parenting 167

SPHERE 4: THE WORLD SPHERE

15. Politics and Religion   181
16. The Acts 4 and Romans 13 Paradigm   189
17. The Humble Boss and Worker   199
18. Humility at Play   211

SPHERE 5: THE SPIRITUAL REALM

19. Authority in Another Dimension   223
20. Victory in Spiritual Warfare   231
21. Live Together, Die Alone   237

Conclusion: A Glorious Ending   249

A Note from Jim   253
Appendix: Group Discussion Questions   255
Notes   261
About the Authors   271

ACKNOWLEDGEMENTS

We want to thank everyone who helped make this book happen. Thank you, Bryana Anderle, for your excellent design work at every level of this book's development. Thanks to Lindy Lowry, Jared Austin, and Logan Malone for your excellent and thorough editorial feedback. Thanks also to Ben Sobels, Julian Vaca, and Cody Macaskill for reading early versions of the manuscript and providing valuable perspective, insight, and encouragement. Jason Jones at Jones Literary, thank you for helping us navigate the best way to get the word out about this book.

Thanks to Luke Yetter and the Relational Discipleship Network for allowing us to partner with your team on this project.

Thank you, God, for your grace and mercy in our lives. We felt you carry us through the writing of this book.

I (Jim) would like to acknowledge the elders and staff at Real Life Ministries, both past and present. We were in it together from the beginning and are still seeking to bring praise to Jesus—the truly humble one!

I (Chad) want to thank my wife, Rachel, for giving me grace and space to work on this book. Thanks also to my dad, Bobby Harrington, and the Discipleship.org team for the invitation to write this book and partner together on this project.

Introduction

A REAL LIFE BATTLE

"Maybe it's time to leave," I (Jim) finally said out loud to myself. For six months, I had seriously considered leaving the church I helped start. Honestly, I never thought I'd say those words.

We had planted the church Real Life Ministries fifteen years before that point, and our church experienced rapid growth in our first ten years—some eight thousand people coming to weekend church services at our peak. More important, around 70 percent of our attendees were in some kind of intentionally relational discipleship group.

When we hit our peak, we began planting churches to reach even more people, instead of adding more buildings to our church. As a result, our people went out to plant churches and our numbers declined at the mother church. It was great for the kingdom, but painful for me because some of my closest friends and coworkers transitioned elsewhere. I was okay with some of this, but I also felt that we had focused too much on planting and not enough on reaching people in our area.

The plateau and decline were part of the reason I was discouraged. If I'm honest, I wanted to lead us to take more ground but felt as if I had to act more like a manager. I wanted us to go through what I saw as an obvious open door to launch a sports and outdoors ministry that would meet a real need in our area. The community had finally approached us to form a partnership! Our community had far too few resources, and the people of our church were passionate to help. I was ready to take ground.

I couldn't see it then, but my pride could have potentially upended my ministry at Real Life. God had a few things yet to show me.

Discouraging and Disappointing Conflict

We have an elder-led church, so I went to the elders and said, "We're losing ground. We need to get moving and figure out how to reach more people in the community."

The elders quickly replied, "No, Jim. We need to solidify the team here and get good processes in place before we take the next hill. We can't keep growing wider; we need to go deeper right now. So we don't want to take new ground."

I pushed back hard, but they wouldn't budge. I don't mind telling you I was extremely frustrated because I believed we could solidify our team while still taking ground. *How could they be unwilling to move forward to expand our reach? Besides, wasn't I the senior pastor?* Most of these men had grown up spiritually under the ministry I had helped create. My pride started to tempt me. I told them that if we continued to decline, we might have to lay off staff.

Discouragement and disappointment marked this whole time. On the personal front, my son had just come out of drug addiction, during which I felt like I had to step back from leading the church in order to focus on my family (which I needed to do). *Now* was the time to refocus, both with my family and with our church. But again, the elders and I were not on the same page.

To make the situation more tense, a divisive staff member decided to start a church down the street with several of his volunteers from his leadership team at our church. He lied to them to get their support, which led to a lot of hurt in our church. This new church started without my knowledge while I was on a three-month sabbatical. When I returned, I was disappointed in how our executive team and elders had handled the situation. In my mind they had been too passive, and the congregation was now confused.

The overall frustration of these individual issues caused us to have many conversations that led some of our elders to conclude I wasn't really listening to them and that I was being too intense. But they weren't really talking to me directly about it, and when I found out about their conversations, I felt hurt. *How could they go behind my back when this was absolutely contrary to the relational environment we had so often talked about and practiced cultivating?*

In the past when conflict had arisen, we had always dealt with issues directly and quickly, rather than going around the person or holding secret meetings. We didn't let conflicts go unresolved. Their actions now were the last straw—I was done. Even though I had taught thousands of people never to leave a church over this type of disagreement—but rather to fight for relationship—this, with everything else, felt like too much for me. What was revealed, from their perspective, was that I wasn't listening, and though they didn't want me to go, they were hurt too.

A Personal Conviction

It just so happened that I had to go on a pre-planned mission trip to India. I told the elders I would be praying about what to do and tell them my plan when I got back. On this trip to India, a very influential national ministry leader and I had a frank conversation after I shared my struggle.

He said, "Is your entire eldership in agreement that you should slow down and work on some issues for right now?"

"Yes, they are," I replied.

"Jim, is it possible you are making irrelevant what they said about your need to change because of *the way* they said it? Are you excusing yourself by hiding behind what you perceive they did?"

Ouch!

Later, he gave me a book he had written about spiritual pride, and let the Holy Spirit do the work. Since my room in India had no television or internet, I had nothing to do but think and read. As I got into the book, I was undone. I realized that while I believed in being coached, being humble, and being held accountable, I really wasn't putting my beliefs into action. I realized that humility is measured by our willingness to submit to authority, even when authority doesn't always "do it right" in our view. Submitting when we don't agree is a test of our humility. I had nearly rejected the authorities God had placed over me. The Holy Spirit revealed the real problem *was with me.* Integrity is a big deal to me, so realizing I wasn't willing to do what I taught just wrecked me. My hypocrisy was clear, and my lack of humility looked me straight in the face: *How had I gotten here without even recognizing it?*

I knew little trust existed between me and the elders, so who would make the first move? Then a simple truth struck me: *humble leaders are willing to go first.* I thought of how Jesus chose to love us first and didn't wait for us to reconcile with him. The truth of 1 John 4:19 hit me like a ton of bricks: "We love because he first loved us." Jesus went first to reconcile with us, and he calls us to go first to reconcile with others as well. Despite my hurt and frustration, I went to talk with my elders.

> *Humble leaders are willing to go first.*

A Turning Point

The elders and I had a big sit-down meeting so I could share what I had decided. I said, "First, I want to work this out with you, but I don't trust you right now, and I don't think you trust me." I shared my frustration about how they had discussions *about me* rather than *with me.* But I also sensed the Lord calling me to take the humble path, so I apologized for not creating a safe environment for them to talk to me. On the spot, we all forgave each other, and then I continued with the humble pie.

"Second, if you all believe it's the right decision to wait on taking more ground, then I will submit to you—whether or not I like it or agree with you. I believe you all love the Lord, and you're not in it for yourselves. I'm going to stay here and work this out with you. I will submit to your authority and do the best I can to follow through with what you think the Lord is telling you." Their heart toward me after this amazed me, and my change of heart dumbfounded them. My confession, this act of humility—which honestly felt more like humiliation in the moment—ended up being a turning point for us all. It led to a massive reconciliation among our elders.

We worked it all out, and I stayed with the church. Eventually, our church even grew to the new heights I had hoped for. The devil had tempted me with pride to destroy our church. But with the help of others—and God—humility set us on a different course as God's team. I knew that strong spiritual leadership requires becoming more Christlike, but I learned in a fresh way that being Christlike includes being the first to act. We so easily put contingencies on our actions without even knowing it: *I will only act if they go first. I will do the humble thing as long as they do it too.* But this is self-seeking. We don't do the humble thing because we'll come out on top but because Jesus, our Lord and Savior, was humble. He taught us to live this way. It doesn't always work out for our immediate good, though. In Jesus' case, it led to his death. That's why true humility is rare. *That's why it's revolutionary.*

Humble Restoration

Like Jim, I (Chad) also needed help to deal with my pride. I was twenty-seven, single, and living at home for a short stint after seminary. It was a tough scenario for everyone involved! To make matters worse, I had a log sticking out of my eye, and I needed help seeing it. One particular eye-opening moment came in a conversation I had with my dad during that time.

A little background: Growing up in a pastor's home, I was very compliant. Even when I was supposed to be rebelling in my teenage years, I didn't. Then, I followed in my dad's footsteps toward ministry and went to Bible college. At that point, we had a great relationship. In my twenties, however, we started arguing regularly. In my eyes, my dad had been perfect my whole life. Then suddenly, I saw his flaws. I was angry, and I took it out on him. I thought, *If my father has flaws, that means I have flaws too. Is it possible for us to change?* Our personal issues combined felt like too much to handle. I didn't want to deal with my flaws—or his.

As a result, our relationship became more contentious. By the time I entered my last year of seminary, our relationship was at an all-time low. What had once been a close father-son bond now hung on by a thread. In fact, I wasn't sure we would have a close relationship again. To add insult to injury, I blamed our bad relationship on him. I couldn't see my part in it. That is, until my dad put it all on the line one Thanksgiving morning.

I walked into the kitchen and saw my dad standing by the counter. We stood talking in the kitchen that morning, and tensions were high as usual. Our conversation quickly spiraled, and I spoke in pride to him. At one point, he asked whether I even wanted a relationship with him. I didn't know what to say. So he finally said, "I want to have a relationship with you, Chad, but I don't need it. I'll be fine without it. But for your sake—whatever is going on with you—you've got to figure it out, or it's going to follow you the rest of your life. You need to honor me and your mother, whether you think we deserve it or not. It's not good for you to act like this."

His words hit me hard. He was willing to let me go my own way if that's what I chose. But in that moment, the sincerity in his face convinced me that he was truly for me. He wasn't in the relationship for himself; he really wanted my good. In this case, that meant my growth in humility with him and others. He knew from life experience what would happen to my character if I didn't deal with this. It would impact every area of my life for the worse.

It was as if the scales suddenly fell from my eyes, and I could see reality. I knew my issue was deep, and while I had blamed our struggling relationship on him, the fault was with me. My attitude toward him revealed my issue. I was focused on his sometimes-rough edges, not the good in him. I had blown his mistakes out of proportion and minimized mine.

In short, *I was proud.*

Our conversation that Thanksgiving morning started me on a different path, and thankfully, during the years that followed, our relationship healed. Now, we are truly reconciled. For us, it wasn't a dramatic reconciliation, like Jim's with the elders, but a slow one. And through it all, I experienced the goodness and peace of humble restoration. While pride threatened to follow me the rest of my life, Jesus showed me a different path: the path of humility. In that sense, my journey is like Jim's and every disciple's journey. We all have the opportunity to walk humbly with Jesus.

Through experiences like these, Jim and I are better able to understand pride because we've seen it deeply in ourselves. We're convinced that pride plagues the church today. Only by learning to walk humbly *in every area of life* can we experience the spiritual revolution we all seek.

> *We can experience the spiritual revolution we seek by walking humbly.*

The Missing Combination

We wrote this book as a guide for walking humbly with Christ in all of life. We write not as leaders who have "arrived" but as fellow travelers with you. So walk with us and learn the humility of Christ as we travel through what we call the Five Spheres of Discipleship:

1. Abiding in Christ
2. The Church Sphere
3. The Home Sphere
4. The World Sphere
5. The Spiritual Realm

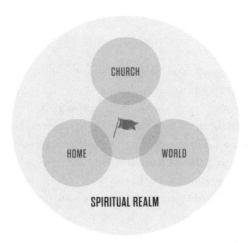

These spheres cover every area of life and frame the discipleship journey for disciples of Christ. In the pages that follow, we will walk with you as we describe each sphere and unpack what humility looks like in each one. Leading up to the spheres chapters, we will share with you our understanding of what humility looks like in the first place. How can we walk humbly in the face of massive cultural changes? We deal with that in Chapter 1. Then, we'll share with you the nature of humble discipleship in Chapter 2, the heart of a revolutionary disciple in Chapter 3, and the core practices of humility in Chapter 4.

You might wonder why we're focusing on the theme of humility. We decided to tie together the five spheres with this theme because it's largely missing from discipleship conversations today. Many people have written about discipleship as well as humility, but we have not found a book, at least in recent years, that addresses both discipleship and humility together. Perhaps this book can help start necessary conversations to address this hole in discipleship discussions today. Even so, we readily admit that what we've written here is just one voice in the conversation.

We're passionate about the theme of humility because we know the intense damage pride wreaks on discipleship, and we're desperate to see the church succeed at her core mission on earth—making disciples. We've seen it time and again: without humility, discipleship is dead in the water. Pride keeps would-be disciple makers passive by luring them to think they are above the call to make disciples. Pride also makes disciples in our churches "twice as much a son of hell" as their disciple makers (Matt. 23:15). But that's only when pride takes over. While pride kills discipleship, humility makes it sing.

> While pride kills discipleship, humility makes it sing.

I (Jim) have been on a personal quest in ministry to lead our church toward maturity in Christ by making discipleship our main goal in all we do. In fact, we have also made discipleship the goal of the Relational Discipleship Network, which trains disciple makers to shift their church culture toward disciple making. I have found the five spheres language we use in this book immensely helpful among leaders.

The idea of walking humbly in these areas is not ours, though. It comes from Paul's letter to the Ephesians as he describes following Jesus in every area of life (what we call the five spheres). As we'll see, Ephesians provides a solid map to navigate our journey through the spheres. I (Chad) have treasured Paul's letter to the Ephesians over the years because I believe it provides a unique message for the church that all generations need to hear. For these reasons we've selected Ephesians for this book because more than any other of Paul's letters, it provides the clearest roadmap for understanding God's heart about the church and how we are to live as God's people within the church. As we'll see, Paul progresses seamlessly from sphere to sphere, touching on every major area of life.

Why do we need to address this issue of humility today? Because most Christians have been converted but not discipled. Even for those who were discipled, their discipleship experience seldom goes beyond doctrinal training or information transfer. Biblical maturity in Christ, however, is something we live out in every area of our lives. Pride gets in the way, so we must walk "with all humility," as Paul says in Ephesians 4:2 (ESV).

I (Jim) worked with my team to develop the five spheres framework from training disciples and disciple makers with leaders in our church and around the world. I have increasingly used it in recent years when I train leaders in our church and beyond because more than any other framework, it transforms the way people view *the scope of following Jesus.* Christians can easily compartmentalize their lives and limit Christ's work to certain spheres, but in Ephesians we're called *to all humility.* This means God gets total control. God wants us to love him with everything we are, in all areas of life. Through the five spheres framework, we've seen God open people's eyes in powerful ways, and we believe God can use it powerfully in your life too.

In this book, we will share with you what we've learned from other leaders, authors, and disciple makers, but most of what we've learned comes from God himself. He has formed us, and as you've already witnessed, it hasn't always been pretty. We've fallen short time and time again. So just like our lives are flawed, we know this book is not perfect. But because we anchor our words in the Word, we believe our message can reliably help you walk through the tumultuous times of today with strength.

We've written with Christian leaders in mind, but the principles of this book can help all disciples think clearly about their progress through each stage of the discipleship journey. We hope this book will help you take significant steps as a disciple of Jesus. Pride presents a real-life battle for all of us, which is not just "out there" but also in our hearts, in our families, and in our churches. If we can win on these fronts, then by God's grace we can win on all fronts.

Guide Your Group Through
The Revolutionary Disciple

Leaders need tools to build up the body of Christ, and we want to equip you to help your church, group, or ministry with easy-to-use tools so you can process the message of this book together. So we've created a suite of free resources to accompany this book. Access these resources by going to TheRevolutionaryDisciple.com/tools. This suite of resources includes message outlines, slides, and ready-to-use graphics for a six-week teaching series.

Also, make sure to utilize the discussion questions we created to go with this book for your church's discipleship groups (see the Appendix). In as few as six weeks, your groups can go through the Introduction and the five spheres of this book. Go to TheRevolutionaryDisciple.com/tools to learn more and gain access to these resources.

1

IS IT TIME FOR ANOTHER REVOLUTION?

At the young age of eight, Josiah took the throne as the new king of Judah. By the time he turned twenty-six, he'd realized there was a major problem in the world, and *he was a part of that problem* (2 Kings 22:1–20). To his credit, he had no father (his dad had been assassinated when he was young), and he had no real relationship with God at that point. He was not set up for success. Yet the people of God needed his leadership. They were in political trouble, and the world stage was abuzz with enemies, posturing, and wars. Josiah didn't know what to do "out there," but he knew, even as a young man, that the external, political unrest probably had something to do with the home front. So he spiritually cleaned house—quite literally!

He told his servants to clean out the temple, which represented God's presence at the time. The temple was in shambles and had become a monument to the gods of their culture instead of the one true God. During this clean-up, the high priest Hilkiah discovered the Torah scroll, which was the Jews' entire Bible at the time.[1] Very few of their Bibles existed at the time, so essentially no one even knew what the Bible said. You can imagine what a discovery this was!

You might ask, *How could they have lost the entire Bible of their time?* It's a historical moment that shows it's possible to lose God's directions amid cultural chaos all around. They had the religion and tools they needed, but they did not personally know God's Word.

Hilkiah read the Bible to Josiah, and once Josiah heard it, he tore his clothes. This was a sign of humility and sorrow in their day. He was undone with conviction because he realized what he and God's people had been doing wrong: they had built their lives on the wrong foundation. They needed to change.

As a result, Josiah reordered the Jews' entire way of living. He started by confessing the wrongdoing of God's people on behalf of everyone because they had "not obeyed the words of this book" (2 Kings 22:13). Then he gathered the elders of Judah so they could all hear God's Word. They recommitted themselves afresh to God. Next, Josiah led the people in repentance and removed the idols of worship from the temple, fired the pagan priests, and removed the Asherah pole from the temple. Scripture tells us that Josiah himself broke down the shrines at the city gate that were dedicated to other gods. He pulled down the altars, smashed them, and threw them into the Kidron Valley. He utterly turned the city upside down, destroying its memorials of disobedience. Talk about a revolution!

Incredibly, Josiah's humility moved God. So God said to him, "Because your heart was responsive and *you humbled yourself* before the LORD . . . and because you tore your robes and wept in my presence . . . your eyes will not see all the disaster I am going to bring on this place" (2 Kings 22:19–20). Josiah's humble heart turned into action, which changed the course of an entire generation. Because Josiah and the elders humbled themselves by taking dramatic action, God rewrote the next chapter of their story.

We are convinced that like Josiah, we have a unique opportunity to make an impact *on generations* if we will take seriously our slice of history. In the New Testament, Jesus asked his disciples a question that remains: "When the Son of Man comes, will he find faith on the earth?" (Luke 18:8). In light of that question, every generation must ask: *Will we humble ourselves and follow Jesus with radical obedience?* If not, we may see an entire generation of people fall even deeper into the idol of self. But if we will humble ourselves under God's Word *in every area of life*, then we could see a radical shift in discipleship in North America and beyond.

Pride in the World Today

The radical obedience of Josiah is like what we see among many disciples worldwide today. We find it encouraging to see that some Christians in North America, for example, seem to be discovering discipleship in a fresh way, even as church membership falls. But we must rediscover *humility* as a characteristic of maturity if we're going to see a resurgence in true discipleship.

The ways many Christians responded to the COVID-19 pandemic revealed the problem with pride in the North American church. When the pandemic began, suddenly everyone had to pick a side concerning issues like meeting in person versus staying at home and wearing a mask versus not wearing a mask.

I (Chad) never thought I'd see the day when people didn't shake hands or hug to greet each other. For months at a time, most of us stayed home due to government lockdowns. Then when we finally emerged, no one could hide their opinions anymore. You literally wore your view about mask-wearing on your face. For me, this wasn't ultimately a religious question or a science question as much as it was a question about authority. Until this point in recent American history, you could basically hide your beliefs about how to respond to authority structures because there was no sustained domestic pressure or crisis. Then, however, disagreements erupted all across the country about how governmental leaders should handle the virus. Experts defended both sides on nearly every issue. We faced a national crisis, and the church got sucked into its "swirling vortex of weirdness," as a previous mentor of mine calls any intensely complicated situation.

Hear this: disagreements are inevitable and have their place. But what bothered both Jim and me more than anything was how Christians responded to the authorities during this pandemic. The issue we had was not whether Christians agreed with the seriousness of the crisis, the masks, or the vaccine. The issue we saw was one of the heart. The veil on the church in North America and beyond was pulled back, revealing strongholds of pride. Conflicts in our country are obviously not going away, so we as disciples must learn how to handle our disagreements with one another and with worldly authorities in humility.

Where I (Jim) live in North Idaho, I have heard more than my fair share of talk about the Constitution and our First Amendment and Second Amendment rights. I've even heard talk about seceding from the nation or a potential militia uprising—*another revolution*. Now, I understand we are far from what our founders intended and that our country is cutting away its moorings from the past that inspired and fueled our success. We are making big mistakes as a country, and if we continue this downward spiral, we face a dire future.

But here's the deeper issue: Why do Christians more readily quote the Constitution of the United States than the Scriptures of God? This question emerged for me as I sat with a group of Christian men who were discussing what sounded like another revolution if politicians succeeded in suspending Second Amendment rights. After ten minutes, not one person referenced Scripture. *How could this be? Have we become like those in Josiah's generation, forgetting the Word of God?*

Our highest priority as disciples is the kingdom of heaven, which encompasses people from every race, tribe, and nation of those who believe. And our highest set of documents is not the Bill of Rights but the Holy Word of God. I don't think we should ignore the Constitution, but as disciples of Jesus, Scripture takes first place because it holds our King's commands. We need a revolution, there is no question, but what does a revolution look like for disciples of Jesus?

In Chapters 15 and 16 we'll deal with politics more directly, but for now, let's look at our root problem, which goes much deeper and broader than just how we respond to a global pandemic.

Pride in the Church Today

In Josiah's day, like ours, the people of God had drifted toward their own understandings, preferences, and selfish desires: in a word, *pride*. Pride rejects God's authority and God's commands and chooses a different path. We see this in the church today, and it affects discipleship on every level.

So we asked ourselves, *What does pride look like for Christians today?* When we started answering this question, we realized the list was long. Pride shows itself when we:

- Blast someone on social media with whom we disagree.
- Scream and yell in anger at a sports game.
- Reject the promptings of the Holy Spirit to give up a particular sin.
- Float from church to church because we're too busy chasing our dreams.
- Rebuff people who hold us accountable for our actions.
- Play the victim rather than trying to understand or resolve the conflict.
- Defend ourselves when someone gives us constructive criticism.
- Leave a church and divide God's people, wreaking havoc along the way.
- Refuse to forgive others when we clearly need forgiveness from God and others too.
- Judge others for their sins but look past our own.

Pride can surface for a disciple at work, in marriage, among family members, and even within discipleship groups at church. Pride is everywhere and all around us. But nobody likes to deal with the pride within. And try as we may to cover it up, we drag this problem of pride wherever we go.

This problem started in the Garden of Eden when Satan tempted Eve to reject God's command and follow her own desires. Adam and Eve's prideful response accomplished Satan's goal: death for us all. He came "only to steal and kill and destroy" (John 10:10). Satan leverages people's pride to distance them from God and divide his people. He can divide a whole church by starting with one divided heart: a pastor who won't submit to their elders, an arrogant leader who believes their way is better, a group of church members who don't agree with the worship style.

Pride is an insidious and subtle killer that destroys our hearts, which bleeds into our relationships with friends, family, church, and community. Pride is simply self-absorption. It sneaks in when we struggle to forgive someone in our church; it slips into our hearts whenever we gossip to make ourselves look better; and it seeps into our lives when we choose our own comfort over helping others.

As disciples of Jesus, we're supposed to be characterized by humility. Yet Christians are still often known for their pride. We have trouble submitting to our supervisor at work and getting along with our coworkers. We move from job to job thinking only about ourselves, just like when we move from church to church for one that "feeds me." When we reject God's commands and act like this, we're often indistinguishable from people in the world, rendering our verbal testimony useless.

> *Pride destroys discipleship at every level.*

When we give in to it, pride destroys discipleship at every level: If we accept Jesus as Savior but refuse to follow him as Lord, discipleship ceases to exist. If we won't be taught by a disciple maker to obey all Jesus commanded, discipleship crumbles. If we won't go where he calls us, discipleship falls apart. If we have the wrong definition of maturity, discipleship efforts don't accomplish their goal. Bottom line: pride kills discipleship.

When the world looks at Christians, they see our billboards, bumper stickers, and marquees. They see our social media posts, the way we raise our kids, how we act at work, how we function as a church, and how we support our kids on the sports field, but does the world see humility in us? Unfortunately, most of the time "humility" is not the first word that comes to mind for them. This is a problem for the church, and if we don't reckon with it, pride could lead to an even bigger problem for our country. And we Protestants in the United States have a particular propensity toward pride.

Americans, Protestants, and Pride

Simply because we live in the US, we breathe the air of pride. If that seems like too great of a generalization, consider our history, which carries with it stories of rebellion during the Revolutionary War. In a country that celebrates independence, giving praise to disciple-making actions like "surrender" or "submission" can be difficult. In fact, words like these seem counter to the freedom on which the US was founded.

American culture today often glorifies pride. Through media, Hollywood, and even sports, pride is pumped into our homes— sometimes overtly, sometimes subtly. We're told by the self-help industry, and many in the counseling industry, to follow our own hearts, to discover our dreams, and to make our mark in the world. We're advised to pull ourselves up by our bootstraps, to stand out, and never to give up. We're not saying these are all bad mottos. But if we don't temper them, we can become rebellious individualists instead of humble disciples. It goes even deeper for us, though. Consider our Protestant heritage.

Christians sparked the Protestant Reformation to reject unhealthy teachings and leadership in the Roman Catholic Church (and rightly so, in some cases). But today we've gone to the opposite extreme of rejecting *all authority in the church*—to our own detriment. While Protestants separated from Roman Catholics with good intentions, they often did this through unnecessary, even violent, rebellion.[2] They rejected the infallible authority of the pope (and rightly so), but they let the pendulum swing too far by rejecting scriptural forms of authority in the church. As a result, many

Christians today refuse to submit even to simple teachings from their pastor, even though the pastor supports their teachings with Scripture and has been given a clear position of authority by God's Word. Protestants often don't submit *to anyone* because they think, *Only God can tell me how to live!* Instead of submitting to God's leaders, as God expects of us, individual believers have become their own authorities. This ideology is faulty and spiritually dangerous.

So our Protestant and US history books are filled with rebellion and pride. Protestant pride in the US seems to have a unique flare, and it deeply affects the people of God.[3] We need more than a shift in the church. We need a revolution of the heart.

Separating Identities

Believers in the US today are discussing a political revolution. We never would have believed it before, but those conversations are actually happening. Let us discuss this briefly before we go into detail in Chapter 15.

While Christians fall on both sides of this debate about a military revolution, what surprises us is that many of those who seem most eager to fight with harsh words or weapons are found in churches on Sundays. It's one thing for a believer to be forced to protect themselves, but it's another thing to go looking for a fight—one that destroys our enemies, when Jesus came to save all people. It makes sense when *non-believers* quickly use violence to make their point, *but Christians?* The lengths to which Christians will go to preserve their personal rights is disconcerting to us. They act like *this world* is all we have. Yes, what's happening in our country is very unsettling, and we fear for our children. But we've got to embrace the differences between the kingdom of God and the United States of America.

I (Jim) liken what's happening in our culture to my experience hunting in the woods here in North Idaho. I often do a lot of scouting in the woods before hunting season to find a possible location for a tree stand where I can wait for animals. Some trees are too small to carry the weight of a guy like me, so I look for multiple smaller trees that stand close together. Many times, I've seen what looks like a gigantic tree from a distance, but as I get closer, it's really two mid-size trees that have grown up close together. As they grow over time, however, two trees like this will often spread further apart; one may die or be struck by lightning, while the other remains. For one reason or another, the tree stand no longer has a place to rest because the gap is too big. I have to adjust and move my tree stand to the one that can hold me because the other doesn't hold weight anymore.

Like this tree analogy, there was a time when our Christian and US values grew so closely together that they seemed like the same thing. As you get closer to the tree, however, you see it is really two trees. Over time, they have grown apart and one has become unstable. This analogy only goes so far, though. It doesn't mean we should abandon our country, but it forces us to ask: *Where does our help come from? In whom do we ultimately trust? Who holds our ultimate loyalty?* When I was younger, most citizens *shared* our values. Then the culture shifted so Christian values were *tolerated*. Now many in authority in the US are *hostile* to Christian values.

> *In whom do we ultimately trust?*

I (Chad) remember in my high school days during the early 2000s how I struggled to work out the difference between kingdom and country. As an example, every day the intercom speaker would say, "Please stand for the Pledge of Allegiance." I would dutifully stand to say the pledge, even though I often stood alone. I stood because, in my mind, I was standing for God and his special country—the United States of America. Now I understand that standing still serves its place, but I had gone too far and made God and country one. It was, I believed, my Christian duty to say the Pledge of Allegiance. There's nothing wrong with standing up for the pledge or the national anthem, but what's happening in our hearts when we do this?

I stand to honor my country now, but I do it for a different reason than I used to. I stand because we're called to honor those in authority (1 Pet. 2:17), and it is proper etiquette in our culture. But the United States of America doesn't hold my ultimate allegiance, and my God and my country are definitely not one and the same. My highest allegiance is to Christ the King. Later, when I learned more about God's kingdom, I realized something had been awry in my heart in high school. I had conflated my political identity with my Christian identity. These have always been separate identities to some degree, but we're seeing their separation more clearly now.

I (Jim) agree. For me, when the pledge is recited, I don't offer my ultimate allegiance to a country that is far from what God would have it be, but rather a prayer for the leaders of this country. I pray that they will move back toward the Lord and for our people to come into a saving relationship with King Jesus.

Jesus, the Revolutionary

If you're tempted to think Jesus *can't relate*, then you ought to look again at both his life and his death. Jesus faced great opposition on earth and made his position clear to the authorities: "Am I leading a rebellion . . . that you have come out with swords and clubs to capture me?" (Mark 14:48). The authorities never knew what to do with Jesus. He had disrupted the religious norms of the day but did so without violence. They didn't have a category for Jesus, so he ended up with the other revolutionaries, such as Barabbas.

Barabbas was a true rebel, put in prison with the other insurrectionists because they committed murder during an uprising. Revolutionaries like Barabbas sought justice and religious freedom from the heavy-handed Roman authorities. While the Jews had rebelled against the Romans in the Maccabean Revolt nearly two centuries earlier, tensions remained high between Jews and Romans in Jesus' day. The people wanted freedom from their political oppressors. Jewish rebels tried to overthrow Rome's delegates, especially in and around God's holy city, Jerusalem. People sometimes confused Jesus and his disciples—even the apostle Paul—with one of these revolutionaries (Acts 5:36; 21:38). And the fate of these revolutionaries was often the same: death by crucifixion.

So Pilate naturally placed Jesus next to one of these rebels on the chopping block for execution. Every year, Pilate selected one prisoner to go free, though. This year, Jesus was up for election. Pilate asked the people to choose whom they wanted released: Jesus or Barabbas (Matt. 27:17–26). But the religious leaders convinced the people to free Barabbas over Jesus. The people wanted the insurrectionist rather than their true King.

If Jesus suffered under false accusations as "a rebel," why would he support his disciples starting a political rebellion today? Jesus' early disciples lived under pagan rule throughout the Roman Empire as he did. So how did the earliest Christians interpret and handle this dynamic? Well, as tensions between religion and politics among Jews and Gentiles grew, Rome ultimately won the battle. The Jews were either killed in battle, starved out of Jerusalem, or conquered during the siege in AD 70. But the very last stand of the Jews happened in a place called Masada, where a few hopefuls died by suicide after a long battle with Rome.

After Jerusalem fell, the gospel of Jesus continued to spread around the world, and Christians sought to deal humbly with their Roman counterparts as they made disciples. At times it was very hard, and many Christians gave up their lives when forced to make the decision to obey God or people. However, their willingness to stand up for Christ unafraid—*and with great humility*—led to many converts. Observers were boggled why these Christians were not so concerned about leaving this planet. The result? "The blood of the martyrs is the seed of the church," as Tertullian purportedly said. In the end, even Rome gave way to Christianity.

Jesus introduced a completely different kingdom and invited his disciples to fight a totally different battle. They became revolutionaries but of a different sort than the world had ever seen. They didn't instigate violent insurrections but wielded their power with the Word and fought with their counter-cultural lives. Their whole-life testimonies took ground because they followed the King of all kings— Jesus, the revolutionary. He led the greatest revolution in history, which not only spread throughout the whole Roman world within a few centuries but also lives now throughout the globe.

The fact that I (Jim) am taking this stance might surprise those who know me because in a different life I was a violent person. I wrestled competitively on the wrestling mat for much of my life, which was violent but legal. I also used my skills on the streets *illegally* more times than I can count. In my natural man, I am a fighter, so it may surprise you when I say disciples really need to slow down and consider what Jesus would say about another possible revolution in the US. Jesus wants Christians to fight, but the fight he calls us to is first a spiritual battle, rather than a physical one. We fight by dying to our sinful nature daily as we take up our cross and follow Jesus. So Chad and I believe Jesus wants a new revolution in the US, but it's a revolution of a totally different kind.

Our hope is that a new discipleship revolution will emerge among disciples of Jesus that is characterized *by humility* and results in healthy relationships that fuel Jesus' mission to save the lost world, rather than destroy it. Pride leads to division and death, but humility leads to life and peace. By God's grace, we choose the latter kind of revolution. We want to present to you a path toward this revolution. It's called humble discipleship.

> *Pride leads to division and death, but humility leads to life and peace.*

2

HUMBLE DISCIPLESHIP

As I (Jim) mentioned, I'm a former wrestler. During my early college days, I wrestled for North Idaho College, and I acted as an assistant coach for the summer wrestling camps hosted by the college. Kids and coaches would come from all over the United States to attend these camps. Our head coach, John Owen, was a national championship coach and had earned the title Coach of the Year many times over as well. I went to North Idaho College specifically because I wanted to be on John Owen's team. Whatever I could do to be near him and learn from him was worth it to me, and all the guys on our team felt the same way.

At the camps, we'd have several hundred kids in one gym with coaches spread out all over. John Owen, or J.O. as we called him, would show a certain move to the whole room of kids using a partner, and the kids would break into twos and practice it.

One day, as I walked around helping different kids, J.O. walked up to a junior high kid near me who was huge for his age. The camp was mostly for high school students, but this younger-than-average kid was allowed in because he was obviously extremely athletic and built for the sport. Yet he wasn't correctly practicing the move J.O. had shown everyone.

So I stood there watching this kid *not do* what he was supposed to, and J.O. said to him, "Hey, let me show you what you're supposed to be doing. You're kind of getting it right, but let's tweak it a bit."

The kid looked at J.O. "I don't do it like that. My way works for me."

"Okay," J.O. said and went to help another kid.

I was flabbergasted! How could this kid be so disrespectful to this legend? And how could J.O. just walk away?

So I laid into the kid. "Do you not understand who he is? That guy is one of the greatest coaches in America. I've won the state championship three times and more matches than you'll ever win in your entire life, and if Coach Owen tells me to do something, you better count on the fact that I listen to and do what he says. And you should too."

The kid looked at me and said, "Nope. I don't do it that way. I win with what I do." Then he blew me off too! So I just shook my head and walked away.

Notice the pride in what that kid said. He thought only about his own limited perspective. What he was doing would work in the junior high competition, but as the competition improved, he would fail.

Later, I went to J.O. to try to understand why he didn't push the kid more. He said something I'll never forget: "You can only coach the coachable, Jimmy. Some day that kid will reach his limit and be average, and his wrestling career will end. Or he will decide to learn and grow. That is his decision, but for now, he has hit his limit. And I am not wasting my time with someone who doesn't want to learn when so many here do want to learn."

You can only coach the coachable.

J.O.'s response profoundly impacted the way I coached wrestlers from that day forward—and how I make disciples. At the time, I applied it only to wrestling, but my experience in making disciples over the last thirty years has taught me how to apply the same truth to discipleship. When someone's pride keeps them from following Jesus—the greatest coach in history—and those who make disciples, they're refusing to be discipled. A refusal to follow Jesus and his disciple makers renders discipleship impossible. In the same way, when Jesus told his disciples to make other disciples, he gave them the authority to coach. Those who would become disciples of Jesus would have to submit to God's disciple makers—their personal coaches—as well.

Coaching the Coachable

Most of us intuitively know the importance of humility in other areas of life. If we're studying for an exam, for example, we submit ourselves to learning the material for the test. We submit to the authority of the teacher, who decides what to teach and what to include on the test. If we don't study the teacher's material, we will likely fail. In our professional lives, we submit to the rules of the workplace, such as showing up on time and doing the job. If we don't comply, we might get fired. In sports, players submit to the coach. Even professional athletes never graduate from submitting to their coach's authority. And if a player doesn't respect their authority, what happens? The whole team likely fails—especially if everyone goes their own way.

The opposite is true too. I (Chad) am a dual citizen to the US and Canada. As a Canadian I grew up playing hockey, so I love the true story depicted in the movie *Miracle*, where Herb Brooks leads the underdog US hockey team to victory in the 1980 Winter Olympics. What made them strong was not star players but a team who worked together—under the leadership of their coach.

We easily understand how important good leadership and humble submission are to win in life. So why do Christians today act like humility is optional for disciples of Jesus? We must be humble because Jesus was humble. He was the perfect model of a mature disciple, but many churches today don't even have a clear, biblical definition of "disciple" in the first place, let alone of a "humble disciple." If clarity on discipleship is new to you or if you're a leader who's not teaching the true definition of discipleship, pay special attention to this next section.

Discipleship Requires Humility

From our interactions with churches in North America and around the world, we've seen how many Christians think that "being saved" is as far as discipleship goes. But that's just the beginning of the discipleship journey. When they came to Christ, they didn't realize— or perhaps didn't want to embrace—the fact that along with the gift of salvation comes the invitation to follow Jesus *into maturity*. Discipleship helps us mature. Discipleship includes being a disciple and making disciples of Jesus—both of which require humility.

In light of that, here's our simple definition of a disciple, which my team and I (Jim) use in our work training leaders through the Relational Discipleship Network:

> A disciple is following Jesus, is being changed by Jesus, and is committed to the mission of Jesus.

This definition of a disciple is simple for people to remember and communicate easily, and it comes from Matthew 4:19, when Jesus said to prospective disciples, "Come, follow me . . . and I will make you fishers of men." His call assumes humility at every level.

"Come, follow me"	A disciple is following Jesus
Submitting to Jesus as leader of our lives takes humility. If taking instructions from someone else doesn't expose pride, nothing does!	
"And I will make you"	Is being changed by Jesus
If we want someone to change us, we must be willing to change. God forms us into the image of his Son as we follow him, which means laying down our rights for the sake of others.	
"Fishers of men"	Is committed to the mission of Jesus
Submitting to Jesus' command to go on a mission and teach others to follow him requires humility. He's not trying to help us accomplish our dreams or mission in life. He wants us to join his mission.	

Discipleship requires humility from start to finish, but seeing this is not always easy—especially at the beginning.

When I (Chad) started leading the young adults at my church, I shared with each person my vision for discipleship and asked if they wanted to join. It went well, but one guy who was on the fringe was overly confident in his maturity.

I sat across the table from him at Jason's Deli and cast my vision for the group. "My goal is to help you become mature and equipped as a disciple of Jesus. Is that something you want to be a part of?"

In between bites of his sandwich, without skipping a beat, he said, "I'm pretty mature, but I could use some equipping." He didn't see it, but he was not spiritually mature at the time. It's hard for all of us to see ourselves clearly just starting out. Yet while he was neither mature nor equipped at the time, he jumped in and learned. In fact, over the next few years he submitted to the waters of baptism and has been growing as a disciple ever since then. Eventually, he took my place as the young adults group leader—the same one I had invited him to join a few years earlier.

Recently, we laughed about that meeting at Jason's Deli, and he admitted, "I had no idea what I was talking about when I told you I was mature." He had a vague notion of being a Christian, but he didn't know what it meant to be a mature disciple of Jesus. Only when he allowed people to invest into him was he able to grow. Over time, he came to see how the whole process of discipleship, which never stops, shapes us into mature disciples.

Jesus Gives Authority to Disciple Makers

We've established that by its very nature being a disciple requires humble submission, but let's talk about the authority of a disciple maker. When Christians read and teach the Great Commission to "make disciples of all nations," they tend to leave out the authority piece.

But notice what Jesus said about his authority when he told his first disciples from a mountaintop in Galilee to go: *"All authority* in heaven and on earth has been given to me. Therefore go and make disciples of all nations" (Matt. 28:18–19). Jesus had received all authority from the Father, and he used that authority to commission his disciples—giving them his authority. Perhaps the church does not effectively make disciples today because we've glossed over Jesus' authority. Authority in this context is the rightful power to influence others for good. Track with us how Jesus' authority has been passed down to us through the ages.

1. Jesus' authority is totally unique. Jesus has *all* authority in the universe. This means that he has the right to command obedience over the cosmos. Every person does well to submit to his authority because it's unparalleled and unmatched. No other human will ever have his authority, even though some people act like they're the king of the universe! So we remember that Jesus is the only one with *all authority.* In light of that, we can understand how Jesus gave authority to his disciples. This was completed when his first disciples received the Holy Spirit "in power" just ten days after his ascension (Acts 1:8). Now empowered by the Spirit, the disciples could effectively go and teach all that Jesus had commanded.

2. The original apostles' authority was special and time-bound. The apostles who stood with Jesus and received the Great Commission in Galilee received a special commissioning to go into all the nations. We can follow in their footsteps, but they were all literally called to go to other countries and make disciples. Peter was an apostle to the Jews, for example, and Paul was an apostle to the Gentiles (Gal. 2:7–8). They were uniquely called to specific tasks that were time-bound to establish the church at the beginning of a new world order in which Jesus had inaugurated his reign and now sits enthroned. We can still receive special callings from God, but none of us will be called to add to Scripture or do other tasks that only the first apostles completed. That window has been closed. So Jesus is our highest authority, and his first apostles carried unique authority as missionaries to the known world at the time (Matt. 28:19). But what does all this mean for disciples now?

3. Disciple makers have general authority today. We will discuss in detail the unique authority Jesus gives elders in the church (see Sphere 2), but for other disciple makers, we too carry the authority of Jesus with us. This is the authority to share the gospel and take someone under our wing to disciple them into maturity. Let's unpack this.

The New Testament reveals how Jesus' first disciples, who had received authority directly from him, proceeded to give other disciples authority to make disciples as well: "And the things you have heard me say . . . entrust to reliable men who will also be qualified to teach others" (2 Tim. 2:2). Church history unveils how these early disciples raised up reliable men and women who have taught others through the ages until today. While we don't have their *level of authority*—founding the church and writing the Scriptures—we do have their same *type of authority*—to make disciples. The apostles made disciples, teaching them to obey Christ's commands, and when we issue those commands as written in the Scriptures, we come under the authority of Jesus. The Scriptures are, after all, inspired and authoritative for the church.

Just like parents have a general responsibility from God to raise their biological children, disciple makers have general authority to make disciples of their spiritual children. Making disciples eventually becomes the responsibility of every disciple who continues to grow. Plus, we have the Spirit, who empowers us for mission. So Jesus gave his authority, but he also assured us of his presence: "And surely I am with you always, to the very end of the age" (Matt. 28:20). So when any disciple is trained up and sent out to teach obedience to King Jesus, they have Jesus' authority and the power of his presence by which to make disciples.

So when someone asks by what authority we make disciples, our answer is that Jesus gave us the authority to accomplish his mission with his people, by his Word, and through his Spirit. In this way, we submit to the mission of Jesus, which started with the first disciples and extends throughout the ages. Even when we "go and make disciples," we take the humble posture of a servant because we're submitting to the authority of Jesus' command to go.

On the flip side, however, if we're not personally committed to Jesus' Great Commission to make disciples in the first place, *we're rejecting his authority.* Granted, it's not always a conscious or intentional decision, but when Jesus tells us to do something and we don't obey—it's rebellion, whether or not we realize it. What does this sort of subtle rebellion look like? When we merely want salvation but don't want to obey, when we won't let Jesus change our hearts, and when Christian leaders don't embody the disciple-making values of Jesus—those are subtle rebellions. The bottom line is this: when we won't go and make disciples, we contribute to the death of discipleship. That puts us on the wrong side of the battlelines in this war.

When Jesus calls us to follow him, he assumes some amount of humility in us. It starts with his call to "Come, follow me" and grows in us through our commission to "Go and make disciples." So if both our calling and commission require humility, what happens in between to help us grow in humility?

The good news is that Jesus teaches us how to be humble. In between the commission and the call, he invites us to come and learn humility from him:

> Come to me, all you who are weary and burdened, and I will give you rest. Take my yoke upon you and learn from me, *for I am gentle and humble in heart*, and you will find rest for your souls. For my yoke is easy and my burden is light. (Matthew 11:28–30)

When we started working on this book, we realized this is an important verse for understanding humble discipleship. We'll unpack Christ's words here as we go, but for now, note that discipleship requires us to learn humility *from Jesus.*

Embracing Humble Discipleship

If the calling of humble discipleship overwhelms you, let us encourage you: by God's grace you can do this. It's not too late to "humble [yourself] . . . under God's mighty hand" (1 Pet. 5:6). In fact, because you are human like the rest of us, you'll have to humble yourself before God and others time and time again. It's a way of life for disciples because we all struggle when the monster of pride rears its ugly head. If you're willing to recognize your pride, there's still hope for you!

While we're still on the journey of discipleship ourselves, we want to share with you a few important principles we've found helpful along the way so far.

1. Recognize pride in yourself. As the saying goes, "The first step is admitting you have a problem." You must start by taking an honest assessment of yourself. A proud person is essentially self-absorbed, as we mentioned. While pride is a complex monster, a proud person simply focuses on themselves. Recognizing pride in your heart is not always easy, though, so read these statements and be honest about any proud thoughts that might run through your mind:

> *A proud person simply focuses on themselves.*

- *I don't obey someone unless I agree with them.*
- *I don't trust leaders over my own intuition and instincts.*
- *I don't serve unless people see my service.*
- *I won't serve unless I'm gifted at it.*
- *I won't be taught because I'm the teacher.*
- *I have nothing left to learn because I am the expert.*
- *I won't be a servant unless it leads to being a leader later on.*
- *I will follow leaders only if I understand the reason behind what they are doing.*
- *I hear from God in a unique way that no one understands except me.*

If you recognize any of these thoughts in yourself, that's okay! Jesus forgives and can lead you down the path of humility. If you *don't* recognize any of these thoughts, then another way to see your pride is to identify any tangible areas of resistance to God or others by asking questions like the following:

- *How well do I submit to leaders at my church or in my small group when they ask me to do something specific?*
- *How well do I submit to my spouse? Do I do what they ask or put up a fight at their every request?*
- *Do I do what leaders want but carry resentment in my heart for their asking me to do it?*
- *Do I submit to my boss at work or resist in small ways?*
- *Do I obey the laws of my country or find ways to skirt around them?*
- *When I hear God's voice asking me to obey, do I listen or rebel?*

These questions might surface pride in your life. Again, if you start to see it, that's okay to admit. Welcome to the club! Once you admit your problem, though, you can start embracing the solution.

2. *Embrace humility as a necessary response to the gospel.* One reason people resist Jesus and his delegated authorities is because they never signed up for submission! They accepted a gospel that says Jesus is Savior but not Lord. As a result, the gospel they've believed does not include a whole-life commitment to follow Jesus. So take an honest look at the gospel you believe, in case that's you. Different so-called gospels are out there, but Jesus' gospel leads to discipleship. That's what Bill Hull and Ben Sobels emphasize in *The Discipleship Gospel*: "You can't make a Christlike disciple from a non-discipleship gospel."[4] We must assess the gospel we believe in—and teach others to do the same—to make sure it assumes humble submission. This largely has to do with whether we understand Jesus as the saving King who reigns over creation or just as a sage teacher who helps us into heaven when we die.[5]

3. *Understand God's heart about delegated authorities.* We've mentioned God's "delegated authorities," but we want to be even clearer about this point. Scripture identifies at least seven specific delegated authorities. When we come under a delegated authority, we're ultimately submitting to God's authority. Look at how God clearly asks us to submit to each one:

- God (James 4:7): "Submit yourselves, then, to God."
- Spouse (Eph. 5:21): "Submit to one another out of reverence for Christ."
- Parents (Eph. 6:1): "Children, obey your parents in the Lord, for this is right."
- Church leaders (Heb. 13:17): "Obey your leaders and submit to their authority."
- Believers in general (Eph. 5:21): "Submit to one another out of reverence for Christ."
- Supervisors at work (1 Pet. 2:18): "Slaves, submit yourselves to your masters with all respect."
- Governmental authorities (Rom. 13:1–2): "Everyone must submit himself to the governing authorities, for there is no authority except that which God has established. . . . He who rebels against the authority is rebelling against what God has instituted."

Submitting to each of these authorities is part of following Jesus. We've listed them here as a sneak peek into our journey toward following Jesus with humility *in all areas of life*. We've looked at the critical importance of the discipleship-humility connection, but what does humility look like more practically? There's no better place to look than to Jesus, the revolutionary disciple.

3

THE REVOLUTIONARY DISCIPLE

In AD 44, the ruler of ancient Judea, King Herod, delivered a message to the people. He must have knocked it out of the park because after his speech, people said, "This is the voice of a god, not of a man" (Acts 12:22). *Nice speech.* What happened next, though, is shocking and gruesome. Scripture tells us, "Immediately, because Herod did not give praise to God, an angel of the Lord struck him down, and he was eaten by worms and died" (Acts 12:23). *Not so nice.* The king who had received blessings from God didn't correct the people. Instead, he basked in the glory of his self-perceived importance. As a result, he experienced firsthand what it means to be humbled by God. The early church heard loud and clear: don't be like Herod!

As we look to Jesus for what humility looks like, King Herod's actions offer a clear example of what humility *does not look like.* This account leaves no room for doubting what God thinks about the issue of pride. To God, humility is more important than even living another day (at least on this occasion). Thanks be to God he doesn't strike everyone dead who struggles with pride!

Herod's demise is a gut check for us all about pride. God cared so much about our journey toward humility that he was willing for someone *to die* as an example of what *not to do.* Even more, he was willing to send his Son to die as well to show us what *to do*. Jesus showed us what humble discipleship looks like in life, not just in death, though. His costly example was so revolutionary that it literally changed history.

A Humility Revolution

I (Chad) was encouraged to learn how the life of Jesus changed the world's view of humility itself. In his book *Humilitas*, historian and minister John Dickson recounts from a historical view how Jesus' example not only led to a new way of life but also to a new way of *thinking about humility*. Until that time, Greeks accepted a form of "humility" that meant lowering oneself before *someone who is greater than them*. But they despised humility as we know it today—lowering oneself for someone of equal or lesser position. Dickson's historical research team found that Paul's letter to the Philippians was the first time in Greek and Jewish literature where "humility" was prized as lowering oneself for others of *equal or lesser status*.

Paul uses Jesus' humility to write, "In humility consider others better than yourselves," because Jesus "humbled himself and became obedient to death—even death on a cross!" (Phil. 2:3, 8). From this time on, Western cultures changed from despising to prizing humility, and historians trace this change back to Jesus' example, as recorded by Paul. Jesus quite literally ushered in a "humility revolution."[6] Clearly, Jesus was a revolutionary. But was he a revolutionary *disciple*?

Was Jesus even *a disciple* at all? How can we call Jesus a disciple when he is the Author and Perfector of our faith, our Great Teacher and Disciple Maker? Yet as strange as it might sound, Jesus was a disciple. He "became *obedient* to death" (Phil. 2:8), and "although he was a son, *he learned obedience*" (Heb. 5:8). Disciples learn obedience, thus Jesus was a disciple. So the Bible describes Jesus not only as a Son but also as a student. He was fully divine, yes, but these passages show that when he became human—he limited himself. In so doing, he had to learn what to say and what to do, and he always gave credit for his actions and words to the Father (John 5:19;

12:49–50). We don't pretend to understand how all of this works, but these passages show us that Jesus not only taught us the path of humility but he also walked it. We can be confident that Jesus can reliably help us along the journey.

Learning Humility from Jesus

As disciples, we have the privilege of learning the humility of Jesus—*from Jesus.* And it's more than just learning *about* his humility; we can actually learn *to become* humble like Jesus, the humblest person ever to walk the earth. And although we'll never reach perfection in this life, by his Spirit, we can grow in humility.

Remember that "a disciple is following Jesus, is being changed by Jesus, and is committed to the mission of Jesus." With that definition in mind, here's the first part of how we define a *humble* disciple:

> A humble disciple knows who they are before God and chooses to go lower . . .

Let's break this part of the definition down before we get to the rest.

A humble disciple knows who they are before God. When we're unsure of our identity, we feel the need to create one. We can either create one for ourselves—which leads to pride—or we can receive one from God. In Ephesians, God gives us a clear identity "in Christ." In Christ we are adopted by God, a part of his household, citizens of his kingdom, and part of his body (Eph. 1:5; 2:19; 3:6). We are his "masterpiece" (Eph. 2:10, NLT). As we come to understand who we are in Christ, we can live according to who we are in him, not because we *need to fill a void.*

Self-created identity can drive us to be "the greatest" mom or banker or entrepreneur or pastor or leader or whatever we do—to feel valuable. Don't get us wrong, excellence has its place, but when we try to create our identity instead of receiving it from God, we wind up exhausted with something that doesn't last. We must reject pride in the self-made person. That's why we emphasize knowing who we are *before God*, because he alone knows who we really are.

Knowing who we are before God also means we reject false humility, which is when someone appears to be humble but they're actually proud. Those who tout false humility, even unknowingly, act like less than they are. But they do it so others will tell them how great they are. Some people call this "inferior pride." We have inferior pride when we focus on ourselves in a negative way. Someone like this obsesses with *who they're not* rather than *who they are in Christ*. People who don't know their true identity either say, "*Nobody* needs me," or "*Everyone* needs me." They're two sides of the same coin, equal symptoms of the same sickness.

When we embrace the humility of Christ, however, we know *exactly who we are before God*—nothing more and nothing less. We see a beautiful example of this in John 13, when Jesus took off his outer garment, filled a bowl with water, and washed his disciples' feet. Scripture says, "*Jesus knew* that the Father had put all things under his power, and that he had come from God and was returning to God; *so* he got up from the meal, took off his outer clothing, and wrapped a towel around his waist" (John 13:3–4). Jesus knew who he was—his great power, his final destination, and his amazing origin—*and that's why he served.*

The word "so" in this passage connects his identity with his actions. His power, his past, and his future were from the Father, *so* he served. Make sure you get this because it's truly astounding and runs so contrary to our human thinking: *Jesus' humility came from a clear and accurate knowledge of who he was before God.* Jesus *knew* he was equal with God; he *knew* he had all the power in the world; and he *knew* he was secure in God. He didn't deny any of that. These were all part of his identity. In fact, he could set aside the rights of his high position because he had fully embraced his identity before the Father.

But that was Jesus, you might think. *I can't be as sure of who I am and be humble like he was.* Yet Jesus calls us to be confident in what he's done for us, and as a result we can become humble like him. Paul reiterates this: "Think of yourselves the way Christ Jesus thought of himself [who] . . . didn't think so much of himself that he had to cling to the advantages of that status no matter what" (Phil. 2:5–6, MSG). Jesus knew his identity in the Godhead, and from that place of security he was able to lay down his rights. We are not divine like Jesus, but the principle here applies to us: the more secure we are in our true identity, the more we can lay down our rights like Jesus did.

We often feel threatened when someone challenges our identity, though. In some sense, we think we have to prove to ourselves and to others that we are valuable. In one of my men's groups, I (Jim) have two Ultimate fighters. They have fought and won championships in the brutal sport of UFC (Ultimate Fighting Championship). Every so often, people will recognize them in public and mouth off or get in their faces. In each case, they just smile and walk away. I love when someone asks why they don't respond. They just say, "I don't have anything to prove—I know who I am and what I could do." These guys are firmly aware of their identity and capabilities. Jesus was that way but even more so, and we should aim to be secure like him.

A humble person accepts that God has created them anew in Christ Jesus. They know deeply that they were knit together in their mother's womb for a purpose, marred because of sin, and remade in Christ. We like the saying, "A humble person doesn't think less of themselves but thinks of themselves less often." We'd add that when humble people *do think of themselves*, they seek to see themselves through the eyes of God—which is their true identity.

A humble disciple chooses to go lower. Scripture tells us, "While we were still sinners, Christ died for us" (Rom. 5:8). Jesus didn't wait until we moved toward him; he took the first step. I (Jim) mentioned that God convicted me to take the first step in reconciling with the elders at my church when we had an unresolved conflict. This conviction came through a man—my friend in India—who was led by the Holy Spirit. He saw my pride and pointed me to Jesus. The Holy Spirit confirmed his words in my heart as well. A humble disciple does not wait for the other person to do the right thing but proactively chooses the humble path regardless. They are the first to ask forgiveness, the first to serve, the first to surrender, the first to listen, the first to . . . whatever love looks like in a given moment. They are the first to show it. Our entire lives are to be characterized by being proactive and going first with humility because Jesus "first loved us" (1 John 4:19).

In John 13, Jesus "went lower" by washing his disciples' feet. Normally, a teacher like him would not wash feet, but he decided to take a step down from his high position and take a servant's posture. Even his incarnation was an act of humility because he chose to take the stairs from heaven down to earth. Jesus chose to go lower because that's what humility does.

> *Until humility is a choice, it's not true humility.*

That's why we define a humble disciple as someone who "knows who they are before God and *chooses to go lower*." Walking humbly is a choice. When someone has no authority, it's not a true sacrifice. They may have "humble circumstances," but given the opportunity to take something for themselves, they would. Until humility is a choice, it's not true humility.

Jesus proactively took the lowest place on earth when he "humbled himself and became obedient to death—even death on a cross!" (Phil. 2:8). The cross was a public place of shame and mockery. As if death in human flesh wasn't humble enough, Jesus experienced the most humiliating death possible. At every turn he could have escaped, but he proactively chose death. Because of this choice, we can make the same revolutionary decision to carry our crosses.

Going lower takes the form of simple actions, such as taking the last seat at the table, the last place in line, and the least desirable portion. I (Chad) think of how Mother Teresa made a habit of always taking the worst pair of shoes when a new load of used shoes arrived at her poor community in Calcutta. The world says a person like that is weak, but Christ tells a different story. Choosing to go lower is for the strong, not the weak.

More Than a Feeling

I (Chad) remember learning an important lesson about humility when I was in a class at Ozark Christian College in Joplin, Missouri, with Mark Moore. We were studying the life of Christ, and when we got to the last week of class, which coincided with Professor Moore's teachings about the last week of Jesus' life, he turned a lecture into a very personal real-life experience.

One day that week, we arrived and all the desks were gone from the room. We all took a seat on the floor. Then he walked in with a bowl of water in his hands and a towel over his shoulder. We knew class was going to be different that day.

"We've been together for a few months, and I've gotten to know you both inside and outside of the classroom," he said. "So I've selected twelve students whose feet I'm going to wash today."

He proceeded to wash their feet, one by one. The class roster was fifty people long, so most people sat and watched. As the students took off their shoes and socks—revealing the lint between their toes and their stinky feet—we all realized this was indeed a unique and memorable day. As he washed feet, Mark spoke words of encouragement (or challenge) into the lives of each one whose feet he washed. To make it even more personal, he identified each of the twelve students with one of the twelve disciples of Jesus.

As he moved from student to student, I thought to myself, *Will he pick me next?* I wanted to be chosen because I wanted him to speak into my life.

He finally made it to the twelfth person, and my heart sank. That is, until he called that person "Judas." *Glad he didn't pick me for that one!* We couldn't believe he would do that. He warned this student that while they were not like Judas now, if they weren't careful, they could become like Judas. We all sat with mouths agape, shocked that he would associate one of our classmates with Jesus' betrayer. With that, he finished, and our class session was over—or so we thought.

He dismissed us, and we began to pack up our things. Then in dramatic fashion he said, "And if you're waiting on *feeling* humble so you can act humble, that feeling may never come. I'm much more concerned to see someone *act* humble than *feel* a certain way before they serve people."

Then he added, "And if you're wondering why I didn't wash *your feet*, you missed the point." His point was that humility is not about us or how we feel about ourselves. It's about what we do.

I often think about what he said that day. I can wait on a certain humble feeling, but unless my humility is characterized by action, it's not truly the humility of Christ.

C. S. Lewis wrote about how action leads to transformation in *Mere Christianity*. He shared with us a great discipleship secret:

> It would be quite wrong to think that the way to become charitable is to sit trying to manufacture affectionate feelings. . . . The rule for all of us is perfectly simple. Do not waste time bothering whether you 'love' your neighbor; act as if you did. As soon as we do this we find one of the great secrets. When you are behaving as if you loved someone, you will presently come to love him. If you injure someone you dislike, you will find yourself disliking him more. If you do him a good turn, you will find yourself disliking him less.[7]

God uses our actions to affect our attitudes. It's true for becoming more loving, and it's true for becoming humbler. If we struggle with pride, our actions can train our hearts. But the truth remains that while we can act humble without having a humble attitude, we can't truly have a humble attitude without acting in humility. We need humble action and a humble attitude to have the humility of Christ. We need both because Jesus warned us not to do our "acts of righteousness" to be seen by people but to do them from the heart (Matt. 6:1).

God uses our actions to affect our attitudes.

Plus, Jesus' actions came from his heart. He said, "Learn from me, for . . . I am humble *in heart*" (Matt. 11:29). His heart was the source of his humble obedience. How do *we* do this? We follow Jesus, and God forms our hearts. This isn't a natural process. That's why we need *God to form our hearts* in this way. But here's the catch: God often forms us *as we obey*. So many people use faulty reasoning about this, for instance, when it comes to financial giving. They say, "God loves a cheerful giver, and since I'm not cheerful, I won't give." *Wrong!* As we choose to be obedient and change our thinking about money, with the Lord's help, we become what we choose. In all areas of life, we obey from the heart and let feelings come, if they may.

God Forms a Humble Heart

By this point, you're probably feeling convicted. As we look at the humility of Jesus, we all fall short, so conviction is sure to come. The good news is we have Jesus as our model, the Father as our source of identity, and the Holy Spirit as our helper. So we don't have to figure out how to manipulate our thoughts to make us humble people, and we don't simply need to "pull ourselves up by our bootstraps." Jesus sympathizes with our weaknesses and invites us to "approach [his] throne of grace with confidence, so that we may receive mercy and find grace to help us in our time of need" (Heb. 4:16). When—not if—we fail, we become aware of God's grace in our lives. This propels us to go further in our journey rather than stop in failure. We *want* to be like Jesus because of how great he is to us.

While action plays a significant role, let us be clear: it's not about our actions alone. God works in our hearts. Yet we must still accept his invitation and approach his throne. So God's work in our hearts and through our actions is motivated, energized, and directed by God from start to finish. Jesus shows us this path of discipleship; we simply learn from him as we walk with him.

If your heart is not truly committed to this journey, you'll likely stop serving as soon as people stop watching. It takes an inward posture of genuine humility to live like this, so trust God with your heart because he's the one who makes us humble. In our experience, he often uses our own obedience to shape our hearts more than anything else (except perhaps life circumstances out of our control). What does this look like practically? In the next chapter, we'll give you four tools to help along the way.

4

THE PROFILE OF A REVOLUTIONARY

When I (Jim) was a boy, I got to see humility in action by watching my dad and mom. My dad in particular often admitted his mistakes, and he made many! He would confess them to me and my family, and even to the whole church. I vividly remember one Sunday when he showed us all what it looks like to act humbly.

He was a church planter at the time, and all seven members of our family would go early to set up church in a school. That day we were in a hurry, and one of the guys on the set-up crew, Bob, made a mistake. My dad lit him up. He yelled at Bob in front of all of us because he was so frustrated. While only a dozen or so people witnessed this, it was an uncomfortable situation to say the least—the pastor yelling at a church member on a Sunday morning.

Before long, it was time for Dad to preach at the service. He stood up to preach, but he didn't talk. He stood in silence for several uncomfortable seconds. *Did he forget his sermon? Was he suffering a stroke?*

Finally, he said, "I can't preach until I make something right." He told the whole church how he had yelled at Bob. He said, "Bob comes early every week to help set up and tear down our church equipment. He serves faithfully. Well, this morning something happened with the chairs, and I yelled at Bob. I humiliated him in front of everyone. I can't preach when I did that to him."

He turned to Bob and apologized in front of everyone. "Bob, I need you to know how special you are and how thankful I am for you. Thank you for coming every weekend and sacrificing your time. I was wrong. Will you please forgive me?"

Of course, Bob forgave him—in front of everyone. Then my dad went right on to preaching. What blew me away was that my dad didn't even talk about it when we went home that day. He just acted like it never happened. He didn't say, "Did you see that, son?" He wasn't doing it to make a point. He was just practicing what Jesus had taught about reconciliation: when you bring your sacrifice to the altar and remember someone has something against you, "first go and be reconciled" (Matt. 5:24).

Whoa. At the time, I didn't understand the significance of my dad's actions. Later, though, I realized my dad had showed great humility that day. I saw what humility looks like as his actions spoke louder than his sermon. My dad's relationships with others have always stood the test of time. Why? Well, when you make mistakes but are consistently humble, it deepens relationships to last a lifetime. Pride harms relationships, but humility makes relationships thrive.

> *Pride harms relationships, but humility makes relationships thrive.*

Looking back now, I realize how my dad and mom modeled humility at home too. How they lived at church wasn't a show; they were the real deal. My mother was consistently humble and even-keeled, so she didn't have to ask for forgiveness as often, but when she was wrong, she pursued reconciliation. My dad and I were both, at times, all over the map, so she forgave us often. She could have proudly said, "I care for you so often in so many ways, yet you run me over again and again." But she didn't. It takes humility to ask for forgiveness as my father had, but it also takes humility to forgive with grace and mercy. We all need people in our lives to show us what humility looks like as we walk together with Christ.

The Core Practices of Humility

Confession is one of the four core practices of humility in the life of a revolutionary. The others are serving, submitting, and listening. Combined, they complete our definition of a humble disciple, which we began in the last chapter:

> A humble disciple knows who they are before God and chooses to go lower *by serving, submitting, listening, and confessing.*

Think of these four actions as the basic rudiments of a humble life, the profile of a revolutionary. They help us march to the beat of Jesus' drum. God calls us to engage these actions because they help us navigate the discipleship journey. In fact, we won't get far without them. So let's talk about each of them in turn so we can easily identify them as we walk through the five spheres.

1. Serving: laying down our desires, preferences, and comforts to physically help others. I (Jim) was reminded of why serving is so important when I was with a church leadership team at a DiscipleShift training event overseas. Before I had spent time with the lead pastor, I was impressed by the strong character of those in his ministry. I noticed that everyone "underneath" the lead pastor was totally servant-hearted.

Learn more about DiscipleShift training events and register at rdn1.com.

So I asked some of the other leaders why they were such eager servants.

"We teach from the very beginning that leadership is servant-hood: servant leadership, servant leadership, servant leadership," they told me.

But the longer I observed the pastor and other "high-level" leaders, the more I noticed they didn't actually serve one another, nor did they serve those "below" them either. Wherever the high-level leaders went, they let their team members *serve them*—even by carrying the leaders' Bibles! It became obvious to me that while they had taught servant leadership from the beginning, at some point they ceased to embody servant leadership. Doing menial tasks, such as moving chairs, was beneath them. It almost seemed as if servant leadership was a stepping-stone to true leadership. But only by serving do we prove ourselves to be servant leaders.

This sounds vaguely similar to what Jesus said about the Pharisees, who loved "the place of honor at banquets and the most important seats in the synagogues" (Matt. 23:6). Jesus taught his disciples to take the opposite posture and serve because "the greatest among you will be your servant" (Matt. 23:11). Left to ourselves, we seek accolades. We sometimes move toward seats of honor, thinking we're doing ourselves a favor, when we're actually feeding the monster within us. Jesus warned us, "Whoever exalts himself will be humbled, and whoever humbles himself will be exalted" (Matt. 23:12).

Jesus taught we become humble by serving others, but he modeled it too. After Jesus washed the disciples' feet, he asked them, "Do you understand what I have done for you? . . . You call me 'Teacher' and 'Lord,' and rightly so, for that is what I am. Now that I, your Lord and Teacher, have washed your feet, you also should wash one another's feet. *I have set you an example that you should do as I have done for you*" (John 13:12–15). That's what humble, relational discipleship looks like. Jesus told his disciples to do what he did for them: the shockingly humble service of cleaning dirty feet. Notice, again, he told them *to do something humble*, not merely to think about themselves in a humble way. No matter what position we hold—on a board, on a committee, on a church staff, as an employer, as a coach, etcetera—we never graduate from the humble job of serving others.

How are you at serving others? If you only lead, teach, and organize and never get your hands dirty, you might have a problem on your hands. Jesus told the Pharisees they lacked integrity because they would "tie up heavy burdens, hard to bear, and lay them on people's shoulders, but they themselves are not willing to move them with their finger" (Matt. 23:4, ESV). When we don't model service as leaders, we set a bad example for anyone watching us. Instead, we can show love by giving others what *they need*, rather than what *we want* to give them.

I (Chad) remember what my dad always says: "You can't teach what you don't know, you can't lead where you won't go, and you can't give what you can't show." There's no way around it: humble disciple makers serve others in tangible ways. If you want to grow here, make it your goal to find ways to serve people.

> *Serving is an antidote to pride.*

Serving is an antidote to pride just like giving is an antidote to greed. By serving, you can overcome your selfishness and love people the way Jesus did. So take someone's plate to the sink, empty out the trash, clean the toilet, set up chairs for a church service, or take the last spot in the food line. Find ways to serve, especially when no one is looking. Make service a secret act of worship for you. As you follow Jesus in wholehearted service like this, he will teach you humility.

2. Submitting: coming under the authority of God's delegated authorities. As we mentioned, humble disciples also follow Jesus by submitting to authority. Those who submit like Jesus did, however, seem to be fighting an uphill battle in our culture today. "Submission" has become a bad word because it implies weakness or because those in authority often misuse their power and hurt others. As a result, we attempt to protect ourselves from truly being under *anyone's authority* except our own. We'll unpack this one more in the spheres chapters.

Let's pause here because it's helpful to think of these first two core practices, service and submission, as the two sides of humble *action*. We typically serve others by *giving* them something. We give them a lift, we offer a hand, or we bring them a meal. Submission, on the other hand, is more about *receiving* someone's leadership. Instead of giving through action, we actively receive someone's authority with our deeds. Together they comprise humble action.

Humble listening and confessing complete the four core practices of humility as the two sides of humble *speech*. When we listen to someone speak, we are *receiving* their words, and when we confess, we are *giving* our words to someone else. See how these four practices cover both sides of humble speech and action:

The Profile of a Revolutionary Disciple

	Receiving	Giving
Action	Submitting	Serving
Speech	Listening	Confessing

Taken together, giving and receiving humble words and deeds make for a humble disciple—a true revolutionary. When it comes to the life of a revolutionary, it doesn't get more radical than being humble in everything we say and do! When we live humbly like this, we allow God space to cultivate humility in every area of our lives. Now let's unpack the two sides of humble speech.

3. Listening: seeking the input of others. Proud people never listen to others, but a humble disciple of Jesus listens. Even Jesus listened to the Father. He said, "Whatever I say is just what the Father has told me to say" (John 12:50). Jesus was obedient to what he heard from the Father. So as his disciples, we listen first to God. Scripture says, "The word of God is living and active. Sharper than any double-edged sword" (Heb. 4:12). We receive God's Word, even when it pierces our hearts, and this requires humility. Receiving input from anyone means we recognize our need to learn. Many Christians can quote the passage that says, "All Scripture is God-breathed and is useful for teaching, rebuking, correcting and training in righteousness" (2 Tim. 3:16). But few Christians are adept at receiving Scripture's rebuke, correction, and training in righteousness.

Do we love to receive good teaching? *Yes!* We love more information. But anything that cuts to the heart—not so much. Yet unless we humbly receive the piercing Word of God, we will not be able to progress far on the path of humility. It starts with God's Word, but this principle applies just as much to other people's words to us. Listening to God leads to our being "thoroughly equipped for every good work" (2 Tim. 3:17), and listening to other people generally leads to a humble life. But we shouldn't listen to just *anyone's* input. We must be shrewd and discerning about who speaks into our lives. Yet if we listen to no one, we have a pride issue.

How well do you receive critiques about your work? What about feedback on your parenting? What if someone offers input about how you lead at church? Truly listening to others in these areas requires humility (more on this in Chapter 7).

4. Confessing: freely admitting when we've done wrong. Humble people are not concerned with themselves or how they might appear if they show weakness, so they more naturally confess. This takes two forms: confessing Jesus as Lord and confessing our sins. Confession starts with confessing Jesus as Lord. This includes submitting to his power to say what's right and wrong in our lives. Yet as we follow him, we still miss the mark sometimes. So as his disciples, we confess our weaknesses and our sins too (James 5:16). For example, we might say something wrong, speak inappropriately to a fellow employee, or gossip. When we fail, we confess it and change—all by his power in us. As we abide with Christ, the Holy Spirit convicts us. We confess our sin and receive forgiveness (1 John 1:9). Then we also go to those we've wronged and ask forgiveness from them.

Here's an example of confession. A guy I (Chad) had been discipling for nearly two years started to drift away from our relationship. Eventually we reached an impasse. I don't know if I pushed him too hard or if he wasn't ready to hear what I had to say as I discipled him. Whatever the case, after two years of regularly meeting together, I could see pride in his life. I owed it to him to address it, so I told him that I thought pride was the number-one issue in his life, and he needed to face this reality in order to grow. *Takes one to know one!*

When I would bring it up, though, he got angry and defensive. In fact, one time he got so mad that we had to stop talking on the phone. These conversations didn't go well. In the end, I was disappointed and felt like I had failed. It was a painful experience. He accepted that things weren't working between us, and he decided to leave our discipleship group but stay involved in another ministry of our church.

Even as we ended that season of discipleship together, he started showing signs of humility. He asked what it would look like to grow in humility, so I shared with him the importance of actions like serving and submitting. A lightbulb went off in his head. But instead of looking like an enlightened disciple, he looked more like a deer in the headlights! I knew the feeling. I too had been confronted about my pride, and it's a tough pill to swallow. It feels especially daunting at first. As we finished our conversation, I feared our relationship was essentially over.

Years later, though, we started hanging out again, and our relationship rekindled! One night we were hanging out on my back porch, and he confessed: "I'm really sorry for how I treated you. I was incredibly ungrateful, and I'm sorry." *Wow!* His confession healed a wound in me. I had no idea he even remembered or cared about what had happened. God had been working on him to make him humbler, which revealed itself through his confession. Confession does that for all of us.

This example also shows that God was at work in my friend's life, even when I was not. My friend was meeting with others in the church, and the Holy Spirit continued to form him. This is such an important lesson: we should always avoid being someone's sole disciple maker. Instead, from the beginning, we should make space for other disciple makers. This means that we encourage those we're discipling to seek counsel from others in the church, learn from other teachers, and spend time developing relationships with those who are older and more mature than them. This posture models humility and says, "I don't know everything," which is a form of confession too.

We know that while Jesus didn't have any mistakes or any sins to confess, he did deal with human weakness, which he confessed (Heb. 4:15; Mark 14:34). For example, he wasn't afraid to confess his weakness in the Garden of Gethsemane. That night, Jesus admitted his soul was grieved to the point of death, and he asked the Father for another way. Then he asked his disciples to join him and pray with him. If *Jesus* confessed his weakness and asked for help, then *we* have plenty to confess.

We can sometimes be afraid to confess our sins or mistakes because we think people will judge us. While that might happen, most of the time confession does the opposite. People trust us more. Whether preaching, teaching, or just talking with friends, humble people consistently share their struggles. In this way, mature disciples are honest and transparent. Learning to confess our sins freely helps us also confess our allegiance to Jesus freely. So "confession" means both confessing sin and confessing Christ.

In the last chapter, we emphasized the inner life of a humble disciple: someone who knows who they are and makes the choice to act. This inner life combined with these four actions of humility gives us the full picture. Humility involves the whole person—our heart, our actions, and our words—and it moves from the inside out. We'll flesh all this

> *Humility involves the whole person.*

out more in the five spheres, but for now, remember that we learn the heart of Christ by choosing to serve, submit, listen, and confess.

Moving Forward

If our definition of a humble disciple is right—*a humble disciple knows who they are before God and chooses to go lower by serving, submitting, listening, and confessing*—then it provides a practical way for pursuing the humility of Christ. Jesus modeled these core practices to show us how to grow. We aren't left wondering how to become humble, and we don't continually have to wince as we ask God to make us humble. These practices help take the mystery away. *Becoming humbler is possible!*

We will never be flawless in this life, but as students of Jesus, we can become more like our teacher, who was perfectly humble. Instead of just wandering on the path of discipleship, we can intentionally pursue these actions of Christlike humility and participate with God as he transforms us. These actions have the power to radically alter our lives—and the world. From our experience, as you continue following Jesus in these ways, you will increasingly find that *his* humility becomes *your* humility. This is the kind of discipleship revolution that God wants. With these tools in our hands, now we're ready to walk through the Five Spheres of Discipleship.

Identify Areas of Personal Growth

Here are additional resources to help you process what we've covered so far. The first is a worksheet called "Identifying Pride in the Five Spheres." While this might feel intimidating at first, understanding our problem with pride can liberate us and help us walk in freedom. Identifying areas of growth is a vital step for making progress on our journey as disciples of Jesus. This worksheet provides questions for each of the five spheres to help you recognize areas of potential growth due to pride. You can download this resource at TheRevolutionaryDisciple.com/tools.

The second resource is called "Understanding Submission in the Five Spheres," which is a one-time, stand-alone Bible study for you or your group. It walks you through a biblical understanding of submission to God's delegated authorities, focusing on the seven specific passages we mentioned in Chapter 2. This will help you understand the context of these seven passages as you process God's heart about submission. Download this resource at TheRevolutionaryDisciple.com/tools.

Bridge

WALKING THROUGH THE FIVE SPHERES

Up to this point, we've been describing spiritual growth in terms of *walking on a journey*. Scripture uses this metaphor to describe our experience of growing with God. The prophet Micah writes that God wants us "to act justly and to love mercy and *to walk humbly* with [our] God" (Mic. 6:8). Jesus' first followers literally walked with him on the roads of ancient Israel. Jesus called himself "*the way*" (John 14:6). And Paul describes our whole journey in Christ by saying "*we walk* by faith, not by sight" (2 Cor. 5:7, ESV). So walking is a common image in Scripture for discipleship.

In fact, Paul uses this walking imagery eight times in his letter to the Ephesians. In the middle of Ephesians, he urges them "*to walk* in a manner worthy of the calling to which you have been called, *with all humility* and gentleness, with patience, bearing with one another in love" (Eph. 4:1–2, ESV). So we're literally called *to walk with all humility*. The NIV translates this, "Be completely humble and gentle" (Eph. 4:2). That sounds like a tall order—because it is! But remember that discipleship is always energized by and covered in God's grace.

Walking with All Humility

"Walk . . . *with all humility.*" Did you catch how radical this sounds? It's not just humility we're called to but *total humility.* How are you doing with being *totally humble?* The struggle is real, right? As disciples, though, a major part of our journey is learning to walk with *all humility.* What exactly does this mean?

First, it doesn't mean we must be perfect. If we had to be perfect, we'd all be disqualified! Our best understanding of what Paul means by the phrase "walk . . . with all humility" is that our lives should be *generally characterized by humility.* He didn't mean we're called to be flawlessly humble in every way, but rather to be generally humble in every area

> Growth in humility
> is possible.

of our lives. Every room in the house of our heart has an open door to God's work in our lives. In five spheres language, it's submitting to God in every sphere. Only through Christ is this possible. By his power, we can become increasingly humble in each of these areas. Growth in humility is possible, while flawless perfection is not.

This command to be totally humble comes right in the middle of Paul's letter to the Ephesians, and it's a crucial shift between two major sections. Paul focuses the first half of Ephesians on *right thinking* and the second half on *right living.* In the middle of all that, we find Ephesians 4:1–3, which contains this command to walk with all humility. Its placement is important: Paul is saying, to paraphrase, "Now that you know how to think about your identity in Christ, you need to walk it out with humility, in a way that lives up to your high calling."

He knows that if people truly understand who they are before God, they may start to feel high and lofty. That's what happened to some in Paul's original audience. They had forgotten that the only thing that made them high and lofty in God's eyes was what he gave them through grace and nothing of themselves (Eph. 2:8–10). Paul's words encourage believers to come back down to earth and live out their high calling by walking with Jesus on the humble path of discipleship.

Great journeys involve more than one person, especially when we travel long distances. The journey of discipleship is the same! We go with God and with his people, the church. Friends in the church walk alongside us, encouraging us as we journey through the abiding in Christ sphere, the church sphere, the home sphere, the world sphere, and the spiritual realm.

The Five Spheres of Discipleship

While Paul doesn't use the label "spheres" for these aspects of life, their concepts are woven into Ephesians. Ephesians uniquely reveals what humility looks like in each sphere. Here's an overview:

Sphere	Passage
1. Abiding in Christ	Ephesians 1:2–2:10
2. The Church Sphere	Ephesians 3:1–4:32
3. The Home Sphere	Ephesians 5:21–6:4
4. The World Sphere	Ephesians 6:5–9
5. The Spiritual Realm	Ephesians 6:10–24

- In Sphere 1, Paul writes about the gospel and who we are in Christ. Our identity in Christ shapes our perspective and behaviors in every other sphere of life.
- In Sphere 2, Paul teaches us how to love God's people, especially by serving and submitting.
- In Sphere 3, Paul describes what family life looks like for a believer.
- In Sphere 4, Paul touches on how disciples should behave at work and other environments where we interact with both believers and unbelievers.
- In Sphere 5, Paul unpacks how a disciple can fight in spiritual warfare against the devil.

When we choose God's way, he not only changes us in each sphere, but he also changes us at every level of each sphere. Talk about total surrender! Like the layers of an onion, we have different layers that need transformation in each sphere.

We sometimes describe these layers in terms of the head, heart, hands, and feet, which also comes from Paul's imagery throughout Ephesians:

- *The head.* Jesus is our new "head" (or authority), and he changes how we think as we allow Scripture to guide us (Eph. 1:22; 4:23).
- *The heart.* Through relationship we learn to love God and others. God's kind of love requires humility of the heart (Eph. 1:18; 4:2).
- *The hands.* God teaches us to use our hands to serve him and others in whatever mission he gives us (Eph. 6:7).
- *The feet.* Our feet take us wherever we go to make disciples. As he changes us, we go into the world and reach people with the gospel (Eph. 6:15).

In these different layers we can see the core practices of humility. When we submit at the head level, this includes what we do with our mouths and our ears—humbly confess and listen. The heart comes after this because the heart is not only the place of our affections but also where we make decisions. As we submit to Jesus' authority (the head), he changes our hearts—which includes our will to act—so we can live according to pure motives. With our hearts in the right place, we effectively serve with our hands and go on mission with our feet.

Help for the Journey

As you walk through the spheres, remember Christ's power inside of you. Paul writes about the great authority of Jesus, who helps you fulfill his Great Commission. He is seated "far above all rule and authority, power and dominion, and every title that can be given, not only in the present age but also in the one to come" (Eph. 1:21–22). How does Jesus' power help us walk faithfully? Paul connects the dots when he says *we share in Jesus' power*: "God raised us up with Christ and *seated us with him* in the heavenly realms in Christ Jesus" (Eph. 2:6).

Do you realize how huge this reality is? It means that those in Christ have the power to be free from the burden of pride's dominion in all areas of life. You can be secure in your high position—secure enough to be truly humble. Why? Because Jesus rules supreme in every sphere. Walk in this truth.

As you do, remember to use the four core practices for making progress against pride—serving, submitting, listening, and confessing. Serve Jesus, submit to his authority, listen to his voice, and confess Jesus is Lord and Savior when you stumble. Do these together with God's people. You'll need these tools at every turn, and as you use them, we believe you'll increasingly see how God can make you humble. If at any point you find yourself stuck, it probably means you've loosened your grip on one of them. With these tools in hand and Christ as our guide, let's start walking.

Sphere 1

ABIDING IN CHRIST

God raised us up with Christ and seated us with him in the heavenly realms in Christ Jesus.

— Ephesians 2:6

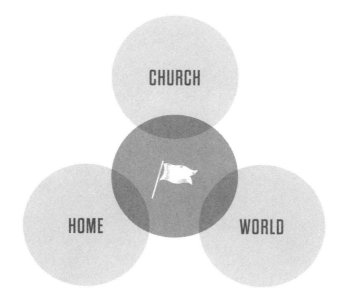

5

THE YOKE OF CHRIST

In 874 BC, King Ahab took the throne in Israel. Scripture tells us he "did more evil in the eyes of the LORD than any of those before him" (1 Kings 16:30). Saying that Ahab did not walk in humility is an understatement. Instead, he flaunted his prideful actions, doing "more to provoke the LORD, the God of Israel, to anger than did all the kings of Israel before him" (16:33).

In contrast stood Elijah, a lone prophet of God at the time of Ahab's reign. He famously called down fire on the prophets of the false gods of their day. He also heard God's "still small voice" and followed God wholeheartedly (1 Kings 19:12). Elijah was discouraged by the lack of faithfulness he saw in King Ahab and among God's people at the time, especially by what might happen when he wasn't around anymore.

But in the midst of all this, we see a beautiful disciple-making moment when Elijah called Elisha to follow him. Scripture says Elijah "passed by [Elisha] and threw his mantle over him" as Elisha plowed his family's farm (1 Kings 19:19, NRSV). This gesture was a clear call to discipleship.[1] Elisha knew he was submitting himself to Elijah, so he slaughtered the oxen he had been using to plow the field, cooked the meat by starting a fire with the discarded farm equipment, and shared the meat with others. Then "he followed

Elijah, and became his servant" (19:21, NRSV). Talk about going all in! He had the submission part of humility down, and he was ready to serve.

Elisha had been going one way, but now he went a totally different way. There was no looking back for him because he had said goodbye to his old life. He knew that accepting Elijah's mantle was no small decision. It signified a total change in his allegiance: he now submitted to Elijah, and ultimately to God.

In the same way, Jesus calls us to follow him by offering us his yoke: "Take my yoke upon you and learn from me, for I am gentle and humble in heart, and you will find rest for your souls" (Matt. 11:29). When we accept Jesus' yoke, we become his servants. We had gone one way, but now we go a different way. Now we work for him—*with him*. We died to the old life and now walk in newness of life. We surrender our agenda to him because we wear his yoke. It's as though Jesus says to us what Elijah said to Elisha: put down your old life, burn it up, and exchange it for the new one I am giving you.

> *When we accept Jesus' yoke, we become his servants.*

The Yoke of Christ

The first sphere of discipleship is abiding in Christ. Before we can successfully journey through the other spheres, we must learn to walk humbly with Christ himself. We do this by taking on the yoke of Christ.

We normally think of a yoke as a burden. So why does Jesus use this word positively? And what exactly does it mean to take his yoke upon us? Plus how does it lead to rest? While Jesus issued this invitation thousands of years ago, it extends to everyone who would learn from him. We know the famous call to follow Jesus from Matthew 4 and the Great Commission to go make disciples from Matthew 28, but why do so few people actually go and successfully make disciples? We believe it has to do with submitting to Jesus' yoke.

When we truly embrace the yoke of Christ in Matthew 11, we enter the classroom of Christ, where we take our first steps in walking humbly with Jesus.

The Light and Easy Path

As we mentioned, the last three verses of Matthew 11 are important verses for this book. Jesus' invitation to "learn" from Matthew 11:28–30 appears nearly halfway through the Gospel of Matthew. It's worth repeating here:

> Come to me, all you who are weary and burdened, and I will give you rest. Take my yoke upon you and learn from me, for I am gentle *and humble in heart*, and you will find rest for your souls. For my yoke is easy and my burden is light. (Matt. 11:28–30)

When Jesus says, "Learn from me," he includes learning humility.[2] What a crucial message for the church today! Embracing this call to learn humility is a major missing element from many discipleship efforts in our time. Learning it well can launch a discipleship revolution.

I (Jim) am convinced that most preachers think they're *teaching* during a Sunday morning church service, and most people think they are *learning* during a worship service. Of course, this is often true to some extent, but Jesus' method of teaching extended far past a mere transfer of information. Information alone doesn't change lives; teaching in relationship does. Jesus taught information, but what he really taught was how to love God and others in genuine relationship. So as disciples, love is something we teach, but we must also learn what love looks like and how to model it. We do this in relationship with Jesus and others. I like to say we learn relationship through relationship.

I appreciate what John C. Maxwell writes in *Developing the Leaders Around You*: "The best type of training takes advantage of the way people learn. Researchers tell us that we remember 10 percent of what we hear, 50 percent of what we see, 70 percent of what we say, *and 90 percent of what we hear, see, say, and do.*"[3] It's funny to me that researchers go to such great lengths to uncover truths like this, only for us to discover that Jesus' way of making disciples shows us the same methods. He did *create us* after all! Shouldn't he know the best way to teach us? We cannot divorce the person of Jesus and the teachings of Jesus from the methods of Jesus and still expect to get the results of Jesus.

Taking on the yoke of Christ also means embracing Jesus' way of life. We greatly desire to put our unique mark on whatever we touch. We're tempted to shift everything just a bit to show we did something special, but that doesn't get us very far on the path of humility.

> *We honor Jesus when we imitate both his character and his actions.*

I love what my friend Brandon Guindon often says: "God didn't ask us to innovate but to imitate." An over-emphasis on innovation creates what he calls a "shiny object culture" in our churches, where people chase after the newest fad. He writes about this in *Disciple-Making Culture*: "Rather than chase these shiny objects, we should focus on creating and living out a healthy culture that creates 'imitators,' as Paul calls them" (1 Thess. 1:6).[4] We honor Jesus when we imitate both his character and his actions.

Matthew 11: Abiding in Christ

We can glean three key takeaways from Matthew 11 about abiding in Christ.

1. Discipleship is relational. Jesus invites us, "Come to me." This is very similar to his invitation to the disciples back in Matthew 4:19 ("Come, follow me"). Jesus' first disciples learned directly from him. While we don't have Jesus on earth today as they did, we can still learn from Christ through his Spirit within us. That's what Sphere 1 is all about: abiding in Christ.

2. Discipleship is work. That is, following Jesus takes work. It is first God's work on our character, but also our work as we engage with him daily. We must pick up our cross and follow him, or we cannot be his disciples (Luke 9:23). When Jesus says, "Take my yoke upon you" in Matthew 11, he invites us *to work.* We typically think of a yoke as a harness around an animal's neck, but a yoke in Jesus' time often represented the work of a slave. Slaves and other workers wore yokes as they worked the land. The yoke helped them distribute the weight of manual labor evenly and efficiently across their shoulders.[5] Often, a teacher's instructions were called "their yoke," and in the case of the Pharisees, their yoke was a bad thing (Matt. 23:4). Jesus redeems this image by casting a different vision for what work means. In the end, Jesus says, to paraphrase, "We're going to be doing some work here!" So it's still work, but it's a different kind of work.

3. Discipleship is restful. While Jesus gives his disciples a heads-up about the labor, he ends with good news: "And you will find rest for your souls." We find rest because in Christ we're no longer fighting against God. He tells us, "For my yoke is *easy* and my burden is *light.*" Do you understand what Jesus means here? Let's look at the connection between work and resting in Christ more closely.

The Restful Work of Christ's Yoke

When Jesus says, "My yoke is *easy,*" he doesn't mean our work ranks zero on the difficulty scale. The Greek word here means our work *won't be too much to handle.* Of course, it doesn't always feel this way. Jesus himself seemed to have been irritated in his work when he said of his disciples, "How long shall I put up with you?" (Matt. 17:17). And consider how Paul instructs the Ephesians to be humble, "bearing with one another" (4:2).[6] We may have moments that *feel like a burden.* But because we're working with Jesus, we know we will make it through. When it feels like we're barely able to stand it, that's when we lean into him.

The phrase "my burden is *light*" means something similar. Like the phrase, "Many hands make light work," we're still working, but our work can be a joy because we're working *with Christ*. Nothing wears us out like going it alone, yet so many Christians choose this hard and painful path. Jesus invites us to work with him so we can find rest for our souls.

The early church father Clement of Rome called it "the yoke of his grace" (*1 Clem.* 16:17). When we put on his yoke, we find motivation, direction, and energy from God's grace, not merely by our effort (Phil. 2:12–13). As theologian and venerable voice Dallas Willard says, it takes our total faith in God to experience the life-giving rest of Jesus:

> If we wish to follow Christ—and to walk in the easy yoke with him—we will have to accept his overall way of life as our way of life *totally*. Then, and only then, we may reasonably expect to know by experience how easy is the yoke and how light the burden.[7]

> *We find rest in Jesus, even as we labor in him.*

Revolutionaries accept Jesus' way of life *in every area of their lives*. While it's important to accept that discipleship is work, we need to know that his way is restful too. We find rest in Jesus, even as we labor in him.

When We Choose the Alternative

Do you feel burdened and weighted down? Perhaps you're stuck in pride. This is a heavy and lonely burden to bear. Ezekiel says, "Our offenses and sins weigh us down, and we are wasting away because of them. How then can we live?" (33:10). But praise God! Christ invites us to find rest in him.

Here's what I (Chad) find wild: Even if we reject Christ's invitation to abide humbly in him, God can still use our pride to bring us to our knees. That's how much God cares about humility. "God opposes the proud but gives grace to the humble" (James 4:6).[8] We can choose the path of humility, but if we choose pride, we'll be humbled by God too. The choice is ours.

Before you make the choice, consider each outcome. We all know people who choose pride, and it's not pretty. Many celebrities, for example, become proud in their rise to fame. They elevate themselves above the crowd and think of themselves more highly than they ought. Pride takes over, and the rest is history. It's not just them, though; anyone who succumbs to pride fails to acknowledge the many graces of God. They credit themselves with their greatness, like King Herod did. We've all seen how this type of life can end in a fiery crash, a drug overdose, or even a scandal. They didn't see it coming. Few ever do.

But how sweet it is when we willingly make the choice to take the humble path! It leads to more and more grace. The positive side of the proverb is just as true as the negative side. While God "opposes the proud," he also "gives grace to the humble." And his grace is just as real as his discipline! He changes us and gives us peace and joy, and his character becomes our character. That's what happens when we take up the yoke of Christ. Taking up his yoke gets us started on the journey, but that's only the beginning.

6

ABIDING WITH HUMILITY

I n the spring of AD 30, Jerusalem was abuzz with the news about Jesus' death and resurrection. It was Pentecost, and the apostle Peter stood up to preach the gospel. Those who were moved by his message repented and were baptized (Acts 2:38). On this day, the church was born as thousands of believers submitted themselves to Christ and entered the journey of discipleship.

Baptism offers a great picture of humility. We let someone dunk us underwater and give up control over our entire bodies! Through baptism we all, like the first believers at Pentecost, accept the message of the gospel and enter into the domain of Christ by coming under his authority. Baptism is a sacrament, but it also symbolizes our entry into lives of humble obedience. It's

> *Baptism symbolizes our entry into a life of humble obedience.*

God's normative way for us to show submission to Christ. By totally submerging our bodies, we reveal the total surrender of our hearts and lives to the authority of King Jesus. We like how Matthew W. Bates describes this in *Gospel Allegiance*:

> Repentance is best understood as turning away from other allegiances to give unique loyalty to Jesus as king. Baptism

is best construed as the premier initial way to confess and
embody allegiance to Jesus as king.[9]

Allegiance brings together both repentance and baptism because
they both show our humble acceptance of a change in authority over
our lives. Through baptism, we submit to and follow Christ. It's our
entry point into abiding in Christ, where we walk with humility.

Our Seat with Christ

This sphere is called "abiding in Christ" because this is where
Scripture places our new identity as disciples. Christ was exalted
to the right hand of God, and now we are *in Christ*—which means
we're exalted with him too! As Paul writes, "God raised us up with
Christ and seated us with him in the heavenly realms in Christ
Jesus" (Eph. 2:6). This amazing position of power should humble
us. This is an important part of our journey because it's impossible
to be humble without first submitting to Christ.

After we embrace our need to be humble *in Christ*, it's a trick-
le-down effect into all of life. When we align ourselves properly
under God, we more readily find the path of humility in the other
spheres. By spending time with Jesus through Scripture, for example,
we discover who God is and what he can do. And so we see the world
differently: he not only created the world but still holds it together
and has a plan for it (Col. 1:15–18).

Reflecting on who he is through prayer and the Word reminds
us who we are in Christ—but also that *we are not him* (far from it).
Our identity has been established *in Christ*. So we see others through
his eyes rather than our own. People may still irritate us or feel like
an obstacle to us, but to Jesus they are people he loves. He humbled
himself to save them, so why can't we do the same? Suddenly, our
relationships become smoother with our parents, our spouse, our
boss at work, governmental authorities, and even church leaders—
because we've learned to abide humbly in Jesus. When we choose
the opposite path, though, we experience the same effect, but in the
wrong direction.

The Ripple Effect of Rebellion

Life comes at us fast—with marriage, parenting, work, and a million circumstances that make up the stuff of life. *Will we obey God in these situations? Will we do what he asks of us?* We rebel when we disconnect from a trusting relationship with God. Our lack of trust can surface in all sorts of ways: we don't read the Word and stop truly believing what it says; we stop regularly praying for his will, and we cut off people who might tell us something we don't want to hear. When our relationship with God suffers, our other relationships suffer too (1 John 1:6–7). That's why we must first come under the lordship of Christ, which means coming under his authority and serving his kingdom purposes above all else.

For anyone in a church leadership role, how we do in Sphere 1 can be even more complicated—and important. We can get so busy working *for God* that we don't spend time *with God*. "Doing ministry" becomes a way of escaping intimacy with God. That's when we unravel. Our lives come undone when our outward ministry for God doesn't match our inner intimacy with God. Doing God's work without connecting with God's heart causes all sorts of damage to us—and to those we serve.

Learning to Abide in Ministry

I (Chad) remember entering my last semester at Bible college, eager to make a difference in the world. I sought direction about my next steps from my mentor at the time, Peter Buckland, who was a professor at the college. He told me he started full-time ministry at twenty-eight years old.

That's old! I thought to myself. *Why did it take him so long? Surely, it won't take me that long.*

A decade has passed since that time. I'm now in my mid-thirties, and the time for me to enter full-time ministry has still not come. I had opportunities to pursue traditional ministry positions, but due to my sense of calling, I've allowed "ministry" to take a different shape than I had once imagined.

I'm convinced that God did not bring me into full-time ministry when I was fresh out of college because of character issues in my life. The main issue for me was pride. Then, as I discovered my true self in Christ, my vocational direction took an unexpected turn toward non-traditional ministry. I'm a business owner, and while my job isn't on staff at a church, I lead the teaching ministry of my church as a deacon, I disciple others, and I even preach on Sunday mornings a few times a year. On bad days, it's a shot to my pride that I'm still not in "full-time ministry." On good days, I see it as a testimony to how God can use each of us in different ways. My work overlaps with traditional ministry, but it's not what I had once imagined. Whether I've made the "right decisions" or not doesn't matter as much to me as it once did. I've found that God cares more about my character than my calling, and I've learned to find peace in him through that. My security in him helps me prioritize the important work Christ is doing *in me* at the abiding-in-Christ level, over the work I might do *for him*. This mindset has been revolutionary for me in my walk with Christ, and I hope it encourages you.

> God cares more about our character than our calling.

I (Jim) too have often been in the habit of prioritizing work for God over abiding with God, but I come at it from a pastor's point of view. I consistently see other pastors do this too. As I become aware of what is happening in me, it brings me to my knees about my own weaknesses in this area. With pastors like me who sometimes struggle with pride in their ministry work, interacting with others can become a hassle when it should be a privilege. We falsely begin asking ourselves, *What am I getting out of this pastor thing?* Instead, we should remember we do it because of what Jesus has already done for us. This happens when we drift from our connection to Jesus, who is "the vine," our source of life (John 15:1). We need to abide humbly in Christ, which requires heart-level engagement with God.

Consider the story of the prodigal son from Luke 15. Two sons are in the story: the son who stayed home and the son who left. The one who stayed with his father did not have *the heart of his father*. So too we can be with Christ but not take on the heart of Christ. The older son refused to forgive his brother and saw his work as slavery rather than as service. Both sons were proud and unable to abide humbly with their father. At their worst moments, they both considered themselves slaves, not sons (Luke 15:19, 29). Christ calls us to be sons and daughters who serve. The order is important: identity before action. This story reveals that while humbly abiding in Christ involves obedience, we cannot neglect our hearts. The grim reality is that if we don't connect with God at the heart level, we risk burnout—or even dropping out of the journey altogether.

A Glimpse of God's Glory

Consider how important God treated Isaiah's heart-level change in Isaiah's throne-room experience. In Isaiah 6, God brought Isaiah into his throne room, where he saw the astonishing glory of the Lord. Until this moment, Isaiah probably thought he was a good Jew, especially because God had chosen him as a prophet to speak to his people. Isaiah may have even thought well of his ministry, his calling, and his life—*perhaps even taking pride in those things.*

After he got a glimpse of God's glory, though, he was wrecked. He no longer had room for pride. Like Isaiah, any humility we think we have pales when we see ourselves before God: "Woe to me! . . . I am ruined" (v. 5). In the presence of God, Isaiah saw who he actually was, which we said is the first step of humility. Like Isaiah, we must know who we are before God in order to move forward effectively on a mission with God. Isaiah had known about God and had spent time reading God's Word, even praying and fasting. In comparison to other Jews, he would have had ample reason to take pride in his spiritual maturity. But what did God do with him? He humbled his servant by showing Isaiah a glimpse of his holiness.

This vision of God's holiness put everything in perspective for the prophet. Rather than looking at people and thinking he was worthy to stand in the gap between God and humanity, Isaiah felt unworthy. What was God's response to Isaiah's humility? God's angel cleansed Isaiah's unclean lips with a coal, and said, "Now that this has touched your lips, your guilt has departed and your sin is blotted out" (Isa. 6:7, NRSV). Notice how Isaiah had to open his mouth to confess before he received God's solution. His confession takes us back to the four core practices of humility.

When God reveals who we are in light of his glory, it levels the playing field for everyone. Even a "holy prophet" like Isaiah realized that no one is worthy. This is not just because of our past sins but also because of our present flesh. Yet God meets us where we're at and heals us, even with fire, like he did with Isaiah. We can't heal ourselves. Only through the work of Christ does God finish his ultimate work in us.

Humility Precedes Commissioning

Disciple makers, make sure to catch this: Before Isaiah went on mission to the Jews, he had to know his place before God so he could walk humbly on his mission from God. Only after Isaiah experienced God like this did he know how to abide humbly in his presence. *Now* Isaiah was ready to go. He recounted what happened after this experience with God, "*Then* I heard the voice of the LORD saying, 'Whom shall I send? And who will go for us?'" (Isa. 6:8).

That's how it works with us too. When we spend time with God, we better see the difference between us and him. God's mere presence—when we're truly aware of it—humbles us. That's what happens as we abide in Christ. By spending time with God, Isaiah knew nothing was greater than giving his life to the mission of God. When he became keenly aware of his smallness, he saw the bigness of God. In like manner, time with God humbles us, and we understand that he is the ultimate authority over us. As a result, at every juncture, we can then submit to his will over ours. This enables us to continue obeying his directions as we follow him into every relationship—in the church, at home, and in the world.

The following chart shows how these spheres intersect, with us abiding in Christ in the middle of them all (signified by the white flag). This visual helps us see that we abide in Christ in all the spheres.

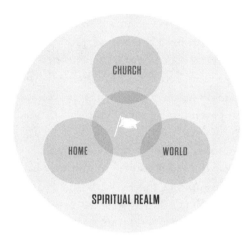

That's how it worked even in Jesus' life. His humility before the Father set the tone for him as he submitted to every authority of life:

- He submitted to the Father in baptism.
- He submitted to the local synagogue (the "church" of his day).
- He submitted to his parents in obedience.
- He submitted to his earthly father by working as a carpenter.
- He submitted to the Romans by paying taxes.
- He submitted to Pilate by dying on the cross.[10]

He did all this because he had first humbled himself under God the Father. Even though he was God's own Son, he was "broken" through the cross. Jesus was the perfect Lamb, and he was still slain. As we abide in Christ, his humility becomes our humility, which always leads us to the cross. And we remember that after the cross comes the resurrection.

Letting Go of Our Agenda

I (Jim) remember how hard it was to lay down my agenda in my early days with Christ. I had so much to lose (or so I thought) if I surrendered. I had become a three-time state champion and a three-time All-American in wrestling. Going into my senior year of college, my dream was to become a four-time All-American. I *had to do this* because my long-term goal was to move into freestyle wrestling and perhaps even pursue the Olympics. Ultimately, I wanted to become a wrestling coach.

At the same time, at the prompting of my dad, I started serving in a church. I was the main youth group leader (still a volunteer at that point). The group had started with four kids and had quickly grown from a small Bible study to a thriving ministry of eighty. Kids were getting saved, and people started telling me, "Jim, you should go into full-time ministry." But that wasn't part of my agenda.

Then halfway through wrestling season, I got mono, which made it impossible for me to do what I had worked so hard for. Mono is terrible for anyone but especially for a wrestler because it drains your energy. Without energy, you can't lose weight and get in shape. My hopes of becoming a four-time All-American were shattered. It was devastating. I remember thinking, *Lord, I'm serving you, and now you're taking away the only thing that gives me credibility.* I had told God that I would give him glory through my wrestling career and had even done that already. Yet in my mind he was taking it all away from me.

Then my dad's words rang in my ears. He had taught me about abiding in Christ from John 15, and I could hear him quoting Jesus' words: "I am the true vine, and my Father is the gardener. He cuts off every branch in me that bears no fruit, while every branch that does bear fruit he prunes so that it will be even more fruitful" (vv. 1–2). Those words cut deep because even though I knew the Lord may have not directly caused my illness, I also knew he was using my illness to "prune" me. This cutting away helps the more fruitful branches, which have the most potential, to grow even stronger.

Pruning literally kills part of a plant so that resources pumped from the roots will be better used in the places that produce the best fruit.

In sports, coaching entails a reshaping of your abilities and character to make you a better athlete. In the same way, Jesus' metaphor about "pruning" describes how God shapes us. What I easily understood from sports, I was now learning on the spiritual front through the help of my dad. God took me out of the sport I wanted to participate in and put me where I needed to be. He cut one thing away from me because he had a better purpose for me instead. The problem was I had a different idea about what the most important game really was. I wanted to fight for God, but my way was not God's way. My dad asked me, "Jim, are you going to trust God, or fight against him and stop abiding in him?"

I would have never made it through that season of life had it not been for questions like that. Using the words of Jesus from John 15, my dad walked with me and continued to help me through challenging church situations too. He also taught me how pray, journal, and listen to those whom God had put in my life to help me spiritually. Through it all, he taught me how to truly and humbly abide with Christ.

The Meaning of "Abide"

Just before his death, Jesus gave his disciples a command he knew was crucial to their future and to the future of the church: "Remain in me, and I will remain in you. No branch can bear fruit by itself; it must remain in the vine" (John 15:4). He told his disciples *to abide in him.*

His disciples were about to face the temptation to leave him. Sure enough, the disciples scattered as soon as their leader was arrested and crucified. This surely wasn't what they had expected. They had anticipated *a real revolutionary*—a triumphant leader, a conquering king—so when they saw Jesus go down, they ran. The disciples had to learn, like we do, that the path of Christ always involves the pain of the cross. They had to recalibrate what a true revolutionary looked like. In those moments, they didn't remain in Christ.

> The path of Christ always involves the pain of the cross.

Maybe you can think about the times in your life when you didn't remain too. It's sobering. If that's you, we encourage you *to remain now*. Soon after the disciples scattered from associating with Christ, they had their resurrection moment with Jesus—quite literally. Through personal encounters with him, they began embracing the full gospel of the resurrected Christ so they could carry out his mission of making disciples. They learned that even when the outlook seems grim—and Satan seems to be winning—Jesus has a plan better than what we can imagine. His plan may not be easy to follow, but from an eternal perspective, it's *so worth it to remain in him*. Although Peter—the same guy who preached at Pentecost—had a rough time in the moment of his great testing, he didn't totally abandon ship.[11] Though he had fled for the moment, he stuck around and learned to remain in Christ. That can be your story too.

Looking back now, I (Jim) was upset that first time I felt God cutting on me. But now I know that for me wrestling was a lesser thing, and it needed to be cut away from my life for me to thrive. God had a different plan for me than becoming a legendary wrestler or a wrestling coach. At the time, though, nothing made sense. That's why I needed my disciple maker's guidance and support. My earthly father taught me that truly abiding in Christ means spending time with Jesus so I can connect with the Father. That was more important than anything I ever *did* for God.

The pivotal moment for both Chad and me was finding our true identities in Christ, and now we can live out those given identities in ways that bring glory to God and eternal significance for us. That's available to all whom Christ saves. Now that we know what it means to abide in Christ and why it's so important, let's talk about the key to abiding humbly in Christ: listening.

7

HUMBLE LISTENING

Come back," I (Chad) said to the man sitting across the table from me. I was eating breakfast with a man from my church. He was about twice my age at the time, so my attempt to bring him back into the fold seemed farfetched. But I thought he might listen to me. He had stopped coming to church after decades of faithfulness to God and family, and he was in the process of leaving it all for a younger woman. Yet somehow he agreed to meet with me.

I had known him since I was in high school, when we worked together on his farm. We had spent hours working his land—planting grass, landscaping, and putting up barbed-wire fences. Now he was living on new land with a new woman. I felt compelled to plead with him. His family was dear to my family, and I was willing to put our relationship on the line.

"I found my soul mate," he told me. I couldn't believe my ears! His "soul mate" was in her forties, and it seemed like she was playing him. From his story I could tell she had flaunted her charm to lure him into an inappropriate relationship. He took the bait—hook, line, and sinker. I listened to his inanities with amazement. *How could this man I've known and respected for so long do something like this?*

"You don't have to do this," I said. "It's not too late." He tolerated my words, but he wasn't really listening. The glaze over his eyes told me that much. His heart was hard because he had chosen the path of pride. Now he wouldn't listen to anyone besides himself. He justified what he was doing too, but it was a fabrication of Christianity, not the real thing based on Scripture.

Our conversation meandered as his delusions multiplied. It ended in the most peculiar way. As we were getting the check, he told me how he wanted to launch a company that sold urns in the shape of a cross. *What?* I thought. *You're living in sin and you're busy thinking about cross-shaped urns?* We paid for our food and went our separate ways. I walked away sad, knowing he was fully entrenched in the "me and Jesus" mentality.

The "Me and Jesus" Mentality

This mentality says we don't need anyone besides ourselves and Jesus to be faithful to God. People with this mindset reject the Word of God for their own idea of how life works. They do this in subtle ways. Instead of doing the hard work of discovering *God's intended meaning in Scripture*, they twist the plain meaning of texts to match their own agendas, preconceived notions of realities, or sin. Perhaps you know people like this, or maybe *you* have this mindset! This insidious mentality left unchecked destroys a person's faith from the inside out—and reveals major immaturity. People like this think they're mature in Christ, but in reality, they're self-deceived. They think they can effectively follow Jesus without committing to a particular church, for example. They don't need to commit to any one team because they're good on their own. And they don't submit to church leaders—even though church leaders are God's delegated authorities, appointed for the good of the body. They're not humble because they're missing the submission piece.

People like this often skirt accountability, rebel against leaders, and avoid all forms of correction. They become deluded by their own thoughts—believing they're hearing from God, when in reality, they're not listening *to anyone*. They continue in their pride because they have no one to walk alongside and help them process their journey. They've accepted the "me and Jesus" mentality, where the only role another believer can play is to nod and accept what they believe Jesus told them.

This can come in an even subtler form too. Perhaps you can relate. I (Jim) see so many leaders who believe their job is to climb to a spiritual mountaintop to hear from God by themselves so they can come down and tell the rest what he said. I'm not downplaying an individual's ability to hear from God, but God expects us to get feedback from other trustworthy people in the body of Christ: "Do not put out the Spirit's fire; do not treat prophecies with contempt. Test everything. Hold on to the good. Avoid every kind of evil" (1 Thess. 5:19–21; see also 1 John 4:1). If God tells us to test what someone else says to help us discern whether their message comes from God, then we must submit to being tested in this way too.

In our recent season of cultural disarray, I (like many pastors) have had to deal with believers who claim to know what God is doing in the realm of politics but who turn out to be false prophets. Just before the 2020 presidential election, for example, many so-called "prophets" came out, stating emphatically that President Trump was going to win the election. These prophets also told us to prepare for battle by hoarding food and weapons. Some people asked me if I believed these prophecies. My answer was always no.

When they asked why, I told them I did not believe these prophecies were consistent with God's Word. God's Spirit never contradicts God's Word. I didn't believe that if worst came to worst, God would want me *to shoot someone* just because they were hungry and wanted my food. When did we get the idea that Christians are supposed to hoard food instead of self-sacrificially give it to the hungry?

> *God's Spirit never contradicts God's Word.*

After election night, November 4, 2020, our country waited for the election results. Early results across every network showed Joe Biden in the lead, but our nation waited for official results. During these days of limbo, I encountered one of these so-called "prophets" at the store. We recognized each other because he had occasionally come to my church. He approached me and told me to let the congregation know that all would be well, that President Trump would indeed win the election with a stunning reversal. God had personally told him to tell other believers this good news so they would settle down.

On the Sunday before the January inauguration of Joe Biden, he walked up to me in the church foyer between services. Instead of humbly admitting his major error, he said this was all just like the story of Elijah—that God was pouring water on the altar so he could perform a miracle. God would come in and appoint Trump to office at just the last minute. As we all know, that didn't happen. There were many conspiracy theories and much vitriol, but in the end, President Joe Biden was inaugurated.

Of course, this "prophet" disappeared for many weeks after the transition of power to a new president. He too had bought into the "me and Jesus" mentality, and he refused to listen to sound reason or Scripture. He was deluded into a religion of his own making, where God's voice sounded a whole lot like his own.

This man's error was not just a mistake but an egregious sin. But this is not new. Even in the prophet Jeremiah's day, God called it out: "How long will this continue in the hearts of these lying prophets, who prophesy the delusions of their own minds?" (Jer. 23:26). We will all answer to God for how we treat the truth. Those who dictate their own terms of discipleship, instead of following Jesus' terms, face judgment just like everyone else. For them, listening to the community of Christ becomes an optional add-on. This is subtle yet seething spiritual pride.

It's Not Just "Me and Jesus"

The opposite of the "me and Jesus" mentality is *humble listening*. When we listen to others in Christ, it's for our good. I (Jim) thank God for the plurality of the leaders I sit under—and alongside. They've kept me many times from driving off the road spiritually. The church is a safeguard for us because even leaders sometimes mistake the Holy Spirit for themselves, which is spiritual pride in its worst form.

The point here is that we don't abide in Christ in isolation, but with the people of God. God's beautiful design here helps us. Our individual relationship with Jesus is a good starting place for interpreting and applying Scripture to our lives, but we need help from others to check and balance our understandings of God's Word and voice. We hope by now you understand this requires great humility.

Not only do we need to learn Scripture together but we also need to be honest about our struggles. When we bring our struggles into the light, we give others the opportunity to encourage us and hold us accountable to do what God's Word says. We also discover how to apply the Word correctly to our individual circumstances. Doing what God asks of us can be difficult, and we need each other. Scripture says, "Whoever isolates himself seeks his own desire; he breaks out against all sound judgment" (Prov. 18:1, ESV). And, "Let a righteous man strike me—it is a kindness; let him rebuke me—it is oil on my head. My head will not refuse it" (Ps. 141:5).

When we truly listen for God's voice, we'll find it often comes through wise people who speak Scripture to us in a way that convicts. How does this work? We must share what we're hearing from God with others through discipling relationships. We all need honest feedback about what we hear from the Lord, which comes through reliable Christians! The Lord often teaches us through others as we share and receive feedback. He also teaches us as we listen to what others hear from God. So while abiding in Christ means spending time alone with God, we do not abide with him alone. We spend time with God among other believers *in relationships* because we need those who are mature within the body to speak into our lives.

Trembling at God's Word

The heart of a humble disciple submits to God's Word and teaches others to do the same. I (Chad) love the verse in Isaiah where God says, "This is the one I esteem: *he who is humble* and contrite in spirit, and trembles at my word" (Isa. 66:2). Notice that when we humble ourselves under God's Word, he "esteems" us. We go low, and God raises us up. I often think about this passage because my parents wrote this verse on the inside jacket of the Bible they gave me when I graduated from seminary. They wanted me to remember that it's not just about Bible knowledge but also about obedience to God's Word from a posture of humility.

I see clearly how this posture toward God's Word is rare today. Few people *tremble* at God's Word in humility. Instead, many assume they know better than God, or dismiss the clear meaning of Scripture. God's Word can be difficult to obey! Plus, it increasingly makes us unpopular in the world. It's easier to seek the approval of people over the approval of God, so some purposely ignore or even reinterpret Scripture to make it acceptable. But someone who *trembles at God's Word* carries a healthy sense of fear that if they don't obey his Word, they're doomed. Revolutionary disciples tremble at God's Word. They know disobedience to him brings real pain. In short, trembling under God's Word means being ready to hear and obey God.

> *Revolutionary disciples tremble at God's Word.*

Single-Minded Obedience

Another way of speaking about this attitude of humility toward God's commands is called "single-minded obedience." Positioning ourselves in humility under God's Word means we obey it no matter the earthly cost. Plain and simple. Obedience is a vital part of being a humble disciple of Jesus. Abiding in Christ means that even before we know what God is going to say or what he'll ask us to do, our answer is yes.

When I (Chad) first read about single-minded obedience in *The Cost of Discipleship* by German pastor, author, and revolutionary Dietrich Bonhoeffer, it made a major impact on me.[12] I realized how radical Jesus had been when he called the rich young ruler, for example, to follow him—and give up everything. This challenged me to the core because I struggled with doubt and living from a divided heart. Embracing the fact that submissive disciples obey with a single mind was hard for me. They have already decided to obey God without distraction or delay. So rather than seeking their own will or the praises of people—or earthly adulation—they set their minds fully on things above. When God speaks, they act. That's single-minded obedience.

Think about raising kids. As parents, we want our children to obey us the first time, right? As soon as we ask them to do something, we want them to jump on it. And if they don't obey right then, it's disobedience. The same is true with God, to whom delayed obedience is disobedience. Our delayed obedience results in unwanted consequences,

> *Delayed obedience is disobedience.*

whether the consequence is a prolonged struggle or a missed opportunity. This happens when we're not abiding with Christ. As disciples and disciple makers, we must continually learn how to hear and obey—which is really one act for single-minded disciples.

That's what the ancient Hebrew word *shema* means ("to hear and obey"). We listen to God not just to gain information but also to obey. This word comes from Deuteronomy: "*Shema*, Israel, the LORD our God, the LORD is one" (Deut. 6:4). Then, in the rest of this passage, God instructed his people to love him with everything they are and to obey his commands. Jesus called this the greatest commandment (Matt. 22:38). To love God with everything we are—heart, mind, body, and strength—means we listen to God and obey him without delay.

Listening to and Obeying God's Voice

Learning to listen to and obey God's voice in one single action is like what happened during the semifinals of the national championship wrestling tournament when I (Jim) was a college wrestler under the leadership of Coach Owen, whom I told you about in Chapter 2. I had made it to the semifinal round, and I had to win this match to advance to the finals. Not only that, but I also needed to win my match to help my team win the national tournament.

I was down by one point with only seconds left on the clock. And until this point of the match, I had been unable to score on my opponent. With only thirteen seconds left, he got a bloody nose, which stopped the clock. We both went to our corners as his team tried to stop his bleeding.

J.O. put his hand on my shoulder. "Jimmy, here's what you're going to do: You're going to do an inside tie, and then immediately drop to a swing single. Then you're going to cut across to a double leg and put him on his butt . . . and win this match—just as time runs out. And because you do that, we're going to win the national title as a team."

In that moment, I felt a rush and realized what was on the line. I thought, *Is that really what I should do? Do I have the strength to do it?* For a few seconds a wrestling match went on inside my head. *Do I obey my coach?*

But J.O. saw in me what I couldn't see because of my exhaustion and frustration. He told me what to do, and he believed I could do it. He had trained me to do it, and I knew what to do. Because he believed it, I believed it too. In that moment, he instilled confidence in me and gave me the courage to act. Right before I went back out, he said, "I've seen you do these moves a thousand times, so I know you can do it. Now go do it!"

So I went *and did it.* I hit the moves and won the match! It happened just like J.O. had said. Even though he had believed in me, I still doubted myself somewhat going into those final seconds. I couldn't see clearly. After all, if I had known what to do, I would have done it already, right? But my coach reminded and encouraged me of my training. I trusted him so much that I went out and did exactly what he had told me to do—no questions, no hesitation. I just listened to and obeyed J.O. because I was already committed to following his instructions even before he told me what to do, even though I had a moment of doubt. I knew he was for me, so when he empowered me to win, he gave me the confidence I needed to be successful.

If that is what we do with a human coach, how much more should we do that with Christ, who has way more power and prestige than my wrestling coach! When we look at Jesus' track record as Teacher and Lord and how he personally saves—even rescues—us from our sins, we know he's for us unlike anyone else. So when he tells us to do something, we say, "Okay, I'll do it!" even before we understand why. We obey him as willing servants who know we're deeply and personally loved by him. Of course, we might wrestle with questions in our own heads, even when we are abiding. But as we reflect on who God is, all he has done for us, and all he knows about us and our situations, we decide to listen and obey—that's simply what humble disciples do.

Now, consider what would have happened if I had *not been willing* to submit to my coach. If J.O. had detected persistent pride in me, he would have cut me from the team long before we ever got to the national tournament. He was the one who controlled who wrestled and who didn't. He would never let someone who doesn't follow a coach's leadership represent him on the team in competition (at least not for long).

In the same way, when we come to Jesus and persistently say, "I want to be on your team, but I'm not going to play by your rules," we cease, by definition, to be his disciples. He won't let us keep playing like that for long. If we persist after many warnings and acts of prodding from God, we effectively choose to be on his team no longer. These are not just our words but the very words of Jesus, who said the Father "cuts off every branch in me that bears no fruit" (John 15:2). Jesus made it clear what he will do with the branches that are withered: spiritual death becomes a reality for those who continually and persistently remain in pride and disobedience.

Sounds intense, doesn't it? But according to Scripture, it's true. We can't fool ourselves into believing that we can be disciples without submitting to God directly and through his delegated authorities. That's like thinking we can be on the team without listening to the coach. It just doesn't work. As we move into Sphere 2, the church sphere, remember that anything we do in the church starts with our submission to God by abiding in Christ. Only from this place of security can we walk with true humility in the rest of life. The world needs this kind of revolution, which starts with disciples who humbly listen to God and to one another. This happens primarily in and through the church.

Craft Your Rule of Life

Looking for a way to grow in Christ? Consider using a tool called "Crafting Your Rule of Life" to help you grow in Christ. The ancient practice of creating a rule of life goes back centuries and stands the test of time, and our tool will help you create your own rule of life. The end result is a personalized one-page bullet-point overview of how you believe God wants you to live your life in Christ. The "rule" part of the name doesn't refer to a set of rules; instead, it's more like the ruler by which you can assess your individual walk with Christ. We all need a clear vision of who we are and who we are becoming, and this tool helps us put that vision on paper.

I (Chad) have adapted this guide from my book *Your Spiritual Formation Plan* to help you craft your own rule of life. Download this guide at TheRevolutionaryDisciple.com/tools. This simple step-by-step worksheet helps you identify exactly how you can love God with all your heart, mind, body, and strength as you seek intimacy with Christ along your journey. When you complete this exercise, you'll walk away with a one-page vision of what your life uniquely looks like loving God with everything you are.

Sphere 2

THE CHURCH SPHERE

Christ is the head of the church, his
body, of which he is the Savior.

— Ephesians 5:23

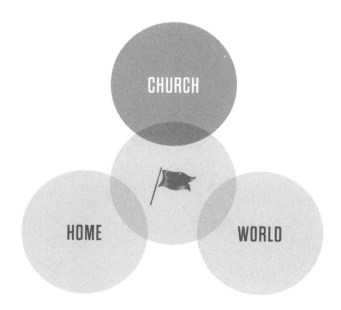

8

IT'S GOD'S CHURCH, NOT OURS

I (Jim) was getting ready to take the stage at a conference to speak about church planting. Just before it was my turn to speak, however, another speaker challenged how church is currently being defined by Christians. He began to tell attendees that each of them did not need to follow current norms; instead, they could start something new. In fact, he said, God has placed a church "within you" and you need to start that church. He went on to say that you do not need a building (I agree), and you do not even need to sing songs or take communion in your church. Rather than having Bible teaching, you and your church can just do service projects together. As he continued, I felt more and more troubled.

Whose church is this? Ours or Christ's? I thought.

Now I have no problem with challenging the norms of church today. I too challenge church norms based on what Scripture reveals. Like with the story of Josiah, radical change comes not by doing away with Scripture but by rediscovering it. The people of God didn't need a new interpretation of the Scriptures to reform the establishment; they needed a new passion for the Scriptures. Once Josiah's crew found the Bible, they were able to compare God's design with

> *Radical change comes by rediscovering Scripture.*

what they had built for themselves. As a result, Josiah led a humility revolution of his own by tearing down all that was added to or taken away from God's plan. Josiah didn't denigrate God's plan; he called the people back to it.

I (Chad) had a similar experience to Jim's, believe it or not. I was visiting the Pacific Northwest, exploring all sorts of ministries to discern if the Lord might be calling me to plant a church there. One church-planting organization was kind enough to let my group of four sit in on their training. The veteran church planter leading the training made his presentation, in which he said God had a specific kind of church for each one of us to plant. He encouraged each of us to dream up our unique church so we could go plant that church— whatever dream was inside of us.

He acted like he was doing me a favor when he came up to me afterward, knelt down, and reiterated his point with a smile on his face. He thought this view would appear attractive to me, but his view actually turned me off to church planting—at least that brand of it. It reeked of sheer individualism and ego to me. I ended up deciding against planting a church at that time for other reasons, but that experience didn't help. This approach felt to me more like a gimmick than God's way. We're not called to "discover the church God has placed in our hearts." *That's bogus!* We're called to discover the church God has *in his heart*. That's the first step we must take to walk humbly in the church sphere: submitting to God's idea of church.

What Is "Church" Anyway?

First, Jesus established *his* church (Matt. 16:18), and *he* appointed *his* disciples not only to spread the message of the gospel but also to establish *his* people as the church. The disciples had caught this vision, which we see play out in the book of Acts. The earliest church, then, shows us the core elements of what "church" meant at the very beginning. This serves as the template for anything we can rightly call church today. So let's start with God's vision for church before we get into how we must live within it.

Keep in mind that the earliest church was composed of disciples who had accepted the gospel and shared a baptismal experience (Acts 2:38–40). Then starting in Acts 2:42–47, we see ten core aspects of church life, what some might call an "ecclesial minimum" (the minimum requirements for what participating in a church means).

The first four are foundational because the first church "devoted themselves" to these aspects of their life together. "They devoted themselves to the apostles' teaching and to the fellowship, to the breaking of bread and to prayer" (Acts 2:42). Have you thought about what this passage means for us today? Let's break it down because many people these days are confused about what "church" means. Scripture guides us into clarity.

1. *The apostles' teaching.* This was the foundation for the church because the apostles' teaching came directly from Christ, who himself was the bedrock of the church (Matt. 16:18). These, in part, are the commands given to the apostles to teach wherever they went (Matt. 28:19).
2. *Fellowship.* The word for "fellowship" here in Acts 2:42 means more than Christians just getting together for coffee and donuts. The early church not only shared their lives in deep, intimate relationships but also their belongings and food.
3. *Communion.* They called it the "breaking of bread" here, but this was shorthand for the sacrament of communion at the time.
4. *Prayer.* Communal prayer characterized the early church. This was likely organized prayer time in some fashion because it's called "the prayers" (ESV), not just "prayer" in general.

Today, we must treasure and teach the words of Jesus, share life together, take communion, and pray together to function as a biblical church. These comprise the core activities of the early church, and they provide guidance for us today about what makes for a biblical church.

The description in Acts 2:42–47 and other parts of the New Testament help us see the importance of six additional aspects, which are vital to any group claiming to be a church.

5. *Gatherings.* The people physically gathered together. In order to experience true and full fellowship, we also must physically gather (Acts 2:46).

6. *Regular meetings.* The believers initially met "every day" (Acts 2:46), but then the early church began meeting weekly on the first day of the week (1 Cor. 16:1–2). While one-time gatherings have their place, a biblical church requires us to have relationships and regular touch-points with others.

7. *Worshiping God.* The early church praised God together (Acts 2:46–47). When we function as God's church, we don't just teach *about God* but we also praise God himself.

8. *Evangelism.* "The Lord added . . . daily those who were being saved" (Acts 2:47). While churches can grow at different rates or have lulls, healthy biblical churches evangelize the lost and grow.

9. *Giving.* As the church grew, they shared physical possessions with those who had need (Acts 4:34–35). They also brought money to their meetings based on their income. Barnabas, for example, gave money he received from the sale of his property so the church could use it as God directed the leaders (Acts 4:36–37). Churches today must help the needy among them and beyond.[1]

10. *Elders.* While new churches don't usually have elders, Paul made sure that churches "in every town" soon had them (Titus 1:5). God still leads his church through a plurality of elders today.

A church can involve more than these essentials—much more!—but not less than these. We can call it a church, but at that point it's no longer a church of God but of our own making. So when we talk about what the church sphere should look like, we're alluding to what *God thinks the church should look like*, not what we think it should look like. We most clearly see this from the first apostles, whom Jesus directly discipled.

No "Minimum" When We're All In

We have to be careful here, though, because if we ask, "What is the minimum we have to do to be considered a church?" and mean "the absolute least we have to do," we're heading for trouble. Rather than looking at what Jesus did—he gave everything—that question asks what we can get away with.

Let's change the scenario to understand this. Say I (Jim) am coaching a kids' ball team, and a player says to me, "Coach, what's the least I have to do in order to be allowed on the team?" As a coach, I would immediately know this kid's heart was not in the game. Let's say a potential new employee says during an interview, "What's the least I have to do on this job?" *Not hired!* Now for something a little more personal: What if I had asked my wife, Lori, to marry me by saying, "Lori, I want to marry you, but what's the least amount I have to do to get you to say yes?" Yeah, it wouldn't have gone very well.

Sometimes we think of church like a buffet. We get to place on our plate whatever suits our taste at the time. *I don't like big groups, so I will only go to a small group,* we think. *I only like one-on-one fellowship, so I will hang just with a few friends—that is good enough for me.* Humble discipleship, on the other hand, allows the Lord to call the shots. It teaches us to say no to ourselves and yes to God. Whatever he says, we are all in—heart and soul. We submit to his ways over ours.

When the minimum ecclesiology topic comes up, people often make church to be whatever they want it to be, or whatever will get people to attend services. I am not against meeting new believers where they are for a time, but we don't have the right to dumb down the requirements for salvation or discipleship by making church what we think it should be. We don't get to change the meaning of church, because it's not ours in the first place.

A true Christ-follower has surrendered to Jesus as Lord and is willing to follow him wherever he leads. Love doesn't seek to fulfill minimum requirements; love gives all. Jesus' original purpose for the church was to make disciples who spread the gospel to all nations via people who love well. He didn't intend our flawed character to discredit the good news by the way we live. He sought to form messengers who had undergone a revolution in their own hearts, who were humble disciples and loved others well.

Love gives all.

What About *These Churches?*

Allow us to be clear about a few important nuances to what we're saying here. People often bring up exceptions by asking, "Well, what about *these types of churches?*" Let's talk about some of the most common ones.

New churches. New churches typically do not have elders, which we listed as vital. New churches are not really an exception; establishing elders just takes time. So new churches can still be biblical churches before they appoint elders, but all mature churches, according to Scripture, eventually have elders who oversee the teaching and spiritual care of their people. So while a church can exist temporarily without elders, if it continues this way, it ceases to be a humble church under God's authority and blessing. A church *must* appoint elders (Acts 20:28; Eph. 4:11).

Home churches. A similar principle applies to home churches. We believe house churches can exist as biblical churches, especially in frontline mission fields, but like any other biblical church they eventually need some form of clearly defined eldership in order to be a mature biblical church. Even those in the persecuted church, who meet in secret or in small groups, must seek elders. They might have to get creative, but since elders are important to God, we can trust that he'll honor our efforts to be faithful to his design for the church as we seek appointing elders.

"Where two or three are gathered" churches. Far too often, we hear people talk about any type of gathering of two or three believers as "church." This is simply *not true*! People quote Matthew 18:20 as a reference point: "For where two or three are gathered in my name, there am I among them" (ESV). But this interpretation is riddled with errors. The most essential error surfaces with a plain reading of the immediate context surrounding this quote. Jesus was talking about church discipline, not what defines a church (Matt. 18:15–20). Since when is Jesus' presence not with us as individuals? He promises, "I am with you always, to the very end of the age" (Matt. 28:20).

The point of including "where two or three are gathered" in Matthew 18:20 was to say that he supports the decision of those who have gone through the process laid out in Matthew 18 for reconciliation. If two or three testify, yet the person refuses to listen, then Jesus promises, "There I am with you," meaning he supports their decision. This passage is not about what composes a church or when God joins a room but what it means to discipline those in the church! No wonder the church today misuses this passage so regularly—it has to do with something that's uncomfortable for us to hear: the authority of Jesus is channeled through church leaders.

Online church service. Almost every church in North America, after COVID-19, can host an online church service, but we must not mistake an online church service for a biblical church. Fellowship can only go so far over the internet. When leaders call for a church to go entirely online or when individuals stay at home to watch service online, we have to ask ourselves why: *Are we staying home because we are sick and don't want others to get ill? Or are we staying at home because we are selfish?* Church is never a one-way transaction, something we only receive. Online church serves a purpose, but we must recognize its severe limitations. How can we physically serve one another, hug one another, and the other "one another" commands in the New Testament if we don't regularly gather in a physical room together? How can we submit to the waters of baptism or receive communion if we don't experience church in person?

What's Missing from "Church" Today

The common missing element in these types of churches—when people define "church" today apart from Scripture—largely has to do with *a rejection of authority*. Why? Reasons vary, but we believe that underneath the surface it has to do with pride. It's not just some of those from younger generations, post-moderns, or progressives who have abandoned biblical church. People of many ages and persuasions are doing it. Rejecting authority, as a root cause, is an ecclesial epidemic that's eating away at the very foundations of biblical Christianity. Increasingly, we've allowed our culture to disciple our minds, and as a result, it's slowly eroding our trust in all basic structures of order and authority:

- We don't trust the authority of God.
- We don't trust the authority of Scripture.
- We don't trust the authority of leaders in the church.

While there are various reasons for all this, we believe the core reason comes back to pride, which is a focus on self. When we *come under anyone's authority* in humble submission, we necessarily reject pride because we're not thinking of ourselves. And when we reject God-given authority in the church, we're rejecting God's authority (Eph. 5:23). So what's missing in so many definitions of church today? *Humility.*

As I (Jim) reflect on the conference I mentioned at the beginning of this chapter, I'm embarrassed to say I got visibly frustrated when it was my turn to speak. But my anger came from my understanding of what humility looks like in the church sphere. Humble disciples allow *God to set the terms of their lives.* We don't come up with *our own* vision for church; we catch *God's vision* for it. He has no obligation whatsoever to bless our watered-down forms of church.

He only claims responsibility to work through *his church*—the way he established it.

The speaker at the conference and the presenter at the church-planter training inadvertently encouraged people to let the enemy redefine church by telling them to start something that feels comfortable and acceptable to them—even if it's not God's definition of church. On the path of humility, though, we choose to lay down our preferences, our comforts, and our rights for the glory of Jesus and for the good of his church. We must wholeheartedly embrace God's definition for church. But there's more. We must also embrace our active participation in the church, even with all her flaws.

9

EMBRACING GOD'S CHURCH

S cripture makes it clear that we're to embrace his church, but that's not always easy, is it? I (Jim) remember when nothing inside of me wanted to accept God's church. Yet God used my dad (my disciple maker) to change my mind and my heart. In fact, I would call it a radical transformation of mindset in my life. My transformation connects to the passage in Ephesians, "Christ is the head of the church" (Eph. 5:23). This experience changed my life forever. Let me give you a little background first.

During college, I had embraced Jesus, but I wanted nothing to do with the church. In my mind, everyone in the church acted like they were perfect with smiles on their faces. Meanwhile, I struggled to get through a day without falling back into alcohol addiction and other issues. I thought nobody was real in the church and nobody was really doing anything to help people like me. But that sort of "reasoning" is often the enemy of humility.[2]

Despite my negative thoughts, I soon came to grips with the fact that you can't have Jesus without the church. Jesus' heart toward the church softened my hard heart toward the church. Even though my dad was a pastor and some of his experiences in ministry presented challenges for me to embrace the church fully, God actually used my dad to help me. It happened through a series of phone calls.

A Wake-up Call

During that season of my life, my dad and I had regular phone conversations. I lived in Boise, Idaho, and he led a church in Montana. During one phone call in particular, Dad's words jolted me and loosened my grip on what I thought of the church at the time. The last time we had talked, I ranted about how I didn't like the church and how they were *just clueless* about what they should be doing and the hypocrisy I felt they exuded. My dad had just listened and made a mental note of it. But when we talked again, he came back to it.

"Jim, I've got an issue in the church, and I don't know how to handle it," he said. "I called to get your opinion on what I should do."

I said, "Well, that's your biggest problem—you're in the church." He was patient with my harsh answer. He just laughed and moved on.

"I've got this family in the church who likes me, but they don't like Mom. They want me to come over and do all this stuff with them, but they don't want me to bring Mom to any of it. What should I do?"

My mom? I thought. *She's the most amazing person on the planet! How could anyone not like her? I could understand having a hard time with my dad, but never my mom.*

Then I said, "Dad, no. Don't go over there. You're married! They can't take you but reject your wife!"

He paused, which he always did when I had cornered myself in some way.

"Jim," he said, "that's how it is with Jesus and the church. You can't have a relationship with Jesus but reject his bride."

Somehow, I was still obstinate, so I pressed him. "Where does the Bible say that?"

He went on to show me God's heart in Ephesians, where Paul describes how God has ordained for us to submit to one another. I could no longer run from God's church because I saw clearly in Scripture that we can't have Christ unless we embrace his church.

My dad's insight and patience changed my life because as I learned to follow Christ in the church, I also experienced how God works through the church. If it hadn't been for him discipling me to embrace the church, I wouldn't have gone into ministry and I wouldn't have learned the importance of committing to God's church. In today's day and age, commitment like this is rare and even radical to some,

> We can't have Christ unless we embrace his church.

but humble disciples embrace the church like this. It's a form of submission and service, two core practices that characterize the revolutionary disciple.

Embracing God's Purpose for the Church

Under Jesus' leadership, church is not optional for disciples. Paul says in 1 Corinthians 12:21 that we *cannot reject the church*: "The eye cannot say to the hand, 'I don't need you!'" Did you catch that? If you're baptized into Christ, you are literally *not allowed* to deny the body of Christ! As disciples, we don't have that right. We depend on each other as different members in the body of Christ, just as much as our hands and eyes depend on each other.

We see this principle in Ephesians too, when Paul says, "To each one of us grace has been given as Christ apportioned it" (4:7). The gifts we have as members of Christ's body come from Christ.[3] The role of leaders is to help equip each part individually and all of us as a group too. God delegated his authority to leaders for the good of his church. So one way we submit to Christ is by submitting to church leaders.[4] Why does he call us to this?

We see the purpose of our submission in the church embedded into Ephesians 4:

> It was [Jesus] who gave some to be apostles, some to be prophets, some to be evangelists, and some to be pastors and teachers, *to prepare God's people for works of service, so that the body of Christ may be built up.* (4:11–12)

Christ has a specific purpose for gifting us with leaders: the building up of the church. How can we build up the church if we're not committed to it? This instructs leaders too. They cannot function as performers or paid players, with the rest of us spectating in the crowd. They are coaches who help place everyone in their positions and equip them to play their role—together. Leaders submit to each other too, so everyone needs this passage about equipping. For all of us, it goes back to our identity. Each of us must know exactly who we are before God in order to humbly embrace the church and our position in the church.

The Purpose of Submission in Church

That's why Paul tells us in Ephesians 4:13 that "we all" (plural) "become mature." Who is the "we" in this passage? It's God's team, the church. How do we become mature? It happens as each part of the body does its work and humbly submits to the authority of church leaders who equip them to do that work. We cannot be equipped in the first place unless all of us come under the leadership, guidance, and administration of God's delegated authorities in the church. The purpose of our submission to one another is service, and the result is maturity, not just as individuals but *as a whole body*.

The Greek word translated "prepare" in Ephesians 4:12 is helpful to unpack. Leaders "*prepare* God's people for works of service, so that the body of Christ may be built up." I (Chad) find Paul's word choice here interesting because this word is also used to describe when fishers *mend their nets*. We find this in Jesus' discipleship call to James and John. They were *preparing* their fishing nets when Jesus called them (Matt. 4:21). In those days, fishing nets would get snags and tears that required repair. So James and John were *fixing their nets* ("preparing") to catch more fish. Since Paul uses this same word in Ephesians 4, we know that a church leader's role in our lives helps fulfill a specific purpose. When we submit to leaders in the church, we're like nets being repaired and mended so we can more effectively join the mission of Christ to fish for people.

Unfortunately, Christians in thousands of our churches today neglect this dynamic of humbly mending and being mended. We need leaders to mend people, and we need people who will submit to being mended. That way we can all help catch and mend others. By God's design, only then can we fully do the good works God has prepared for us. There's really no "me and Jesus" mentality in Christ, like we talked about in Chapter 7. We need to embrace a "*we and Jesus*" mentality instead.

> *We need to embrace a "we and Jesus" mentality.*

Struggling to Commit

With Christ's bride, the church, playing such a vital role in God's mission, you'd think Christians would be more dedicated to it. But from what we see, this just isn't happening today. Why?

We noted earlier that churches are struggling to get and keep members, the main reason being a lack of relational discipleship, in our opinion. Many churches have made converts by promising spiritual "fire insurance" and prosperity but have taught little about what happens next *in this life*—which is discipleship.[5] We believe this is also due, in part, to a widespread and increasing aversion to commitment in our culture. And in some cases, Christians struggle to commit to a local church because they see how the church isn't living up to her high calling to walk "with all humility," as we described (Eph. 4:2, ESV). We understand this struggle.

People feel a need to wait to commit until a church becomes what it's supposed to be. Yet churches will only be what they're supposed to be when we, as God's people, *commit to God's people* and learn to walk through life together. Today, it's so easy for Christians to float from church to church, searching for the one that's doing it "the right way." But when we start pitting ourselves against the bride of Christ like this and elevating our own personal walk with Christ above our walk with his church, we're letting pride creep in. We disobey what the Divine Architect talks so much about—our love for each other, which requires commitment.

How do we move forward? We need to identify any prideful thoughts that enter our minds about the church, such as:

- *If these people would just get it together, we could really do something and be the church.*
- *The leaders at this church just don't get it.*
- *These other people are in it just for their personal gain, but I'm here to serve.*
- *If the leaders don't figure this out soon, I'm going to find another church.*
- *I don't really get anything from church; in fact, I'd be fine spiritually without it.*
- *I could do a better job leading than the leaders of this church. If they knew what was best, they would let me take control.*

We've struggled with some of these prideful thoughts ourselves. So just know that if you struggle with commitment to a local church congregation, we understand where you're coming from.

So many Christians have not been discipled in this area because their parents didn't teach them or because a church they went to didn't prioritize membership. Maybe for you, church was just something you attended rather than something you commited to over the long haul. Or maybe you still have scars that impact your view of church, especially your view of church leaders. But don't let that control how you live. Your hurts can easily develop into a self-protective guard that controls your life, keeping you from all that God could do in and through you.

Committing to a Particular Church

The author of Hebrews pens a striking note about submitting to our leaders in the church: "Obey your leaders and submit to their authority" (Heb. 13:17). Notice this verse says obey *your* leaders, which means they had local church leaders they could identify. Do you see what's happening here? God wants his people to understand that when they commit to the church in general, they also need to commit to a particular local church body. How else can you submit to *your* leaders?

Part of our challenge today is the rugged individualism of our culture. People simply opt out of belonging to a certain congregation. They function more like free agents than as devoted disciples of Christ. Even though churches might define "church membership" in different ways, we can all agree on one thing from Scripture: obedience to Christ requires relationships, and relationships involve commitment to

> *Obedience to Christ requires relationships.*

one another. As disciples, we must settle down, stop jumping around, and commit to a local church.

I (Chad) appreciate how writer Rosaria Butterfield emphasizes this topic in her lectures and writings about the church.[6] She has a unique perspective because she once lived a lesbian lifestyle, but after coming to Christ, she became a homeschooling mom and a pastor's wife—quite a shift of identity!

At a speaking event I attended, she described how same-sex-attracted people often experience extreme ostracizing, which can easily leave people feeling lonely.[7] Also, when she was living in her former lifestyle, everyone in her particular group knew they always had a place to stay each night of the week. Someone's house was designated as the go-to house of refuge for their tight-knit community. She emerged from that community, repented of that lifestyle, and then compared her experience to community in the church. She was grossly disappointed by what she saw and went as far as to say that in her experience, the gay community did a better job at fellowship than the church. She holds out hope for the church, though. I appreciate how she says it in *The Gospel Comes with a House Key*: "Imagine a world where every Christian made a covenant of church membership and honored it."[8] Jim and I believe that vision can become a reality.

Commitment to a local church is only the starting point, we might add. The church has the capacity to have such close fellowship that the world should look at us with awe and wonder. Our radiance can emanate into the world to make people long for what we have. In Christ, we can be the most loving, accepting, and transformational community on planet earth. To become that sort of revolutionary community, though, we must develop long-term relationships with other disciples who are mutually committed to one other. We ought to be committed enough to work through conflict, to be honest with each other, and to allow people to speak correction into us.

Beyond Surface-Level Commitment

So what does this mean for us? It means we stop wandering from church to church, just floating or "church shopping" for the best show in town. Until the Lord sends us out from a church, we should stay at that church. And if we are sent out, our sending should be confirmed by those who know us well and even by the leaders of the church who are sending us. In the rare case that we might need to leave a church for another reason, it should happen in conjunction with the right steps: first try to reconcile any grievances, and then make sure to listen humbly to God's delegated authorities in the church to which you've committed yourself. If you are going to leave and can't reconcile your differences using everything in your power, then leave peaceably without causing division.

Sometimes an unforeseen job change or some other extenuating circumstance will take us away from a church. But in our experience, most people leave a church for the wrong reason or with an unresolved conflict. Whenever people leave in these ways, they cause damage. And some leave without telling anyone. This kind of "ghosting" damages relationships too. Others create a ruckus and a path of wreckage behind them. We've seen how this damage can leave scars. It also reflects poorly on Jesus' reputation. Even when we've been hurt by the body, we're still called to embrace God's church and submit to its leaders. Unless unavoidable life circumstances take us away or leaders ask us to commit obvious sin, the general rule of thumb is to stay at your church. Have you considered how rare yet important this sort of devotion is? One of the most revolutionary acts a disciple of Jesus can make is to stay committed to one church for the long haul.

So often people leave a church because they don't like the direction it's going, but in reality, they simply don't have all the facts. Why? Because they didn't talk to the leaders. We often have conflicting preferences on a certain worship or preaching style, but these are not sufficient reasons to leave our commitment to a church body. Again, if we only submit to authority when we agree with church leadership, is that really humble submission? Just like God hates divorce in marriage, God hates division in his church. As far as it depends on us, he wants us to stay together and work it out.

We stay and work it out because of God's vision for the church. He intended the church to be the central spoke of his missional hub in the world. Paul writes to the Ephesians how God intended that "through the church, the manifold wisdom of God should be made known to the rulers and authorities in the heavenly realms" (Eph. 3:10). The church serves as an important role in the universe. What happens in the church reverberates in the heavenly realms. That is the vision of a revolutionary church. This still leaves one major question for this sphere: What does humble submission to church leaders look like in practice? Let's go there.

10

NAVIGATING SUBMISSION IN THE CHURCH

I n AD 57, the apostle Paul had one last chance to connect with his close friends from Ephesus before completing his third missionary journey.[9] Somehow, Paul knew he would never see his friends, the elders of the Ephesian church, again in this life. They had come out to meet him on the beach, where Paul's boat had docked. He faced likely imprisonment and death at the hand of Caesar. Knowing the gravity of the moment, they all knelt down, prayed, and wept together before saying goodbye.

During this gut-wrenching scene, we get a unique insight into God's delegated authority in the church through appointed elders. Paul said to his friends on the beach, "Keep watch over yourselves and all the flock *of which the Holy Spirit has made you overseers*" (Acts 20:28). This shows that *God* appoints the elders of a church.

As we mentioned, Paul told Titus to appoint elders "in every town" (Titus 1:5). As his letter to Titus continues, we read a list of qualities these men must possess to be chosen as elders (see also 1 Tim. 3:1–7; 1 Pet. 5:1–4). The Holy Spirit helped Titus identify these men, and through this, the Lord gave them authority in the church. The same is true of elders today. God gives elders authority, and they must be qualified and appointed to that position. They serve as God's delegates over the church.

What does that mean for us who are committed to the local body? For starters, we shouldn't resist our elders' leadership unless God reveals these men are the "savage wolves" dressed in sheep's clothing that Paul warned the Ephesian elders about in Acts 20:29. If any of us resists leaders *who are not actually corrupt*, watch out! In this case, we'd be going against the authority of God, who placed them over us. And the Holy Spirit is not a force to be reckoned with (Acts 5:3–6).

We're called to submit not only to elders but also to any church leaders over us. In fact, we're told to "obey" them, as we mentioned (Heb. 13:17). Pretty strong language! But it's clear. Obedience to leaders is not a popular biblical teaching today. Yet our churches desperately need to recover this sense of authority and humble submission in the church. We understand this struggle well, as you know by this point. The command to obey church elders in Hebrews 13:17 and the principle to submit to them can be truly challenging. Our pride, along with the devil's encouragement, leads us to mistrust leaders, do things our own way, and rebel when we don't agree with our leaders' decisions.

Getting into the Weeds of Submission

What does this kind of submission look like? The simple answer is seeking our church leaders' hearts and doing what they ask of us—with big and small requests alike. I (Chad) know that our church leadership, for example, asks us to fill out a "prayer and connect" card every week during the worship service. They've deemed this an important way to care for our church. This card has space for our name and our prayer request. It's important enough that they ask us from the stage *every single week*, so my wife or I fill it out each week. Sure, it's good *for us* that they use these cards to pray, but that's not the main reason we do it. We do it because they ask us to do it. It's a way of submitting to their leadership in a small way. If we refuse to do something like this because we don't agree with it or it's just not our preference, then we're struggling with pride.

That small act might seem insignificant, but what does it say to church leaders when we refuse to do even small tasks they ask of us? Jesus said to be "faithful in little things" (Luke 16:10, NLT). Rebellion in small ways, even if we're unaware of it, is still rebellion. It starts with thoughts like, *I don't need to follow instructions. That's for everyone else, not for me. I'm an exception.* If you struggle with thoughts like these, practice humility by listening for little requests and simply obeying them—even when you don't agree or understand the reason. Remember that God blesses us in our obedience.

I (Chad) was reminded of the unexpected blessings of obedience during the 2020 pandemic lockdowns. My little family of three had planned to relocate from one area of town to another. We sold our house, but our plan to buy another house fell through at the last minute. Yet we still had to move out of our sold house, leaving us only weeks to find a new place to live. On top of all that my wife, Rachel, was very pregnant! Let's just say we were stressed.

Well, Sunday rolled around, and we wrote on the prayer and connect card at church a request about finding a place to live. And would you believe it? Through this simple act, a man in our church read our prayer request and *just so happened* to have a rental property opening right when we needed it. It was amazing: God answered our prayer request *directly through our prayer request!* The house was a perfect fit for us too. What a blessing from God. While I don't always obey my church leaders perfectly, I've found that when I humble myself in small ways like this, the Lord blesses me—and my family too.

We all have opportunities like this to submit to church leaders in small ways, like joining a discipleship group or finding a way to serve when they ask for help. How many times do we find an excuse to prioritize something else over going to small group, service opportunities, and church events that God's delegated authorities over his church have asked us to participate in? They might not ask us individually or directly, but if we're listening for their heart, we see invitations all around. These can be as simple as invitations to attend a church potluck, serve in the children's ministry, regularly attend church services, tithe, or even go to special outreach events. Our participation shows our submission. God calls this good, even when the world calls "submission" bad.

> *Our participation shows our submission.*

We're not saying you must be part of *every single thing* the church asks you to do. We need to have balance and make margin because being *too involved* in your church can be detrimental to other areas of your life. But generally, when your church asks something of you, it's important to prioritize that request. Of course, if church leaders ask you to do something that's clearly sinful, then obey God instead. But most of the time, if we're honest, this issue is just our preference versus theirs. Even if you think your church leaders are asking you to do something against Scripture, you should still make sure you know what's really going on. Are they really asking you to sin here? Or are your leaders simply asking you to do something that gets you out of your comfort zone?

Remember that agreement isn't a prerequisite for submission. If everyone treated their church's requests like a take-it-or-leave-it proposition, our churches would never take ground. In fact, this is exactly how most Christians treat their churches in the US, which is why many churches accomplish so little. But if we would all humbly submit our individual agendas, opinions, and ideas, and simply follow, then we'll truly be able to move forward as a church and take significant ground.

If you're wondering where you stand on this issue of pride in the church sphere, ask yourself: *Do I have a humble posture toward my church leaders, or do I treat everything they say and every request they make as something I'll do only if I feel like it?* Honestly answering that question will likely reveal any pride you might have in this area.

If you're in a church, not currently leading in it, but struggling to submit to your church leaders, consider if the tables were turned! If you were leading, how would you want members to respond to you? You'd want them to follow you, which brings us back to square one. No leader is perfect, so we can't require them to be perfect in order for us to follow them. We hope our leaders are listening to God's voice (and listening to those they lead for ideas and insights as well). But even when they're not fully engaged, that's still no reason to rebel, leave a church, or go off and do your own thing. Often, those who rebel don't have the full story.

Honoring God's Anointed

David was anointed to be king when he was just a boy—not even old enough to fight in battle. But he had to wait at least ten years before becoming king.[10] That was a long time to sit under King Saul, who was unjust and ungodly. Didn't God want David to be king in place of Saul? Wasn't it his right to take the throne? David had the chance to kill Saul in the cave by En Gedi (1 Sam. 24:1–22). *But David refused.* Why? Because of this principle of honoring God's leaders.

Saul was in a bad place spiritually. He had already been rejected by God as king, yet God kept him on the throne for the time being. On top of that, he had even tried to kill David. But David refused to take matters into his own hands because Saul was "the LORD's anointed" (v. 6, ESV). David knew the importance of submitting to God's delegated authorities—even when it was difficult, even when it might cost him his life. This was not weakness but meekness—sometimes called "power under control." The church today needs meek disciples like David who control themselves and submit to God's appointed leaders.

Leaders in the church today don't have the same type of authority the kings of Israel did, but the principle of respecting the Lord's anointed applies to church elders because God appoints them, as we read about in Acts 20. Even church pastors and elders must pay attention to this because no one is king of the castle in the church sphere. Leaders mutually submit to each other, and we all ultimately submit to Christ. Let's remember the first part of our definition of a humble disciple: knowing who you are before God *and choosing to go lower.*

Perhaps you have a position or a place of influence; perhaps you're one of the main leaders of your church. Still, submitting to the elders and other leaders at your church is a choice of taking *a step down* from your positional rights because you know God has delegated his authority to others around you too. Look for authority in the church at every level and how you can come under it. Take it a step further and use your position as an opportunity to serve others, listen to others, confessing any mistakes you might make along the way (whether leadership mistakes or even sin). The truth is when we *don't* make this choice to go lower, we become either rebels or critics—both of which are harmful. Neither builds up the body; instead, they create a negative spirit within the church.

A Parable of Peacemakers

Making the choice to lower yourself can be a real struggle. I (Jim) remember a helpful analogy about the church, which my dad once shared with me during my anti-church season. I was still playing the church critic role. I thought Christians were a bunch of fakes. I didn't relate to Sunday messages, church music, or anything in the church really, and I didn't want to keep going. Then my dad totally turned me around. I was married at the time, so what he said really hit me.

"Jim, I want you to imagine that you're the pastor of a church, and your wife arrives after you one Sunday morning. She pulls up in her own car. When she gets out, she rips her dress on the car door and doesn't know it. The entire backside of her dress is torn, exposing her to everyone at church.

"She walks into the building, and some of the people point at her. Some even snap a picture. Others make fun, and they're not quiet about it either. She hears their jeers and wonders what others are looking at. Some secretly decide in their hearts that she must be inept as a wife.

"One person quietly steps in, takes off his coat, and discreetly walks up to your wife and says, 'You accidentally tore your dress on the way in.' He then covers her with his coat and calmly says to everyone watching, 'Move along.'

"If you were her husband, how would you feel about the guy who did that? Would you feel like he honored your wife? And honored you because he honored your wife? What about everyone else—how would you feel about them?

"In the same way, the church is God's bride. She makes mistakes, and you can either point them out and be critical of them, or you can do something and say, 'I'm going to jump in and do my best to help.'"

Then my dad went further: "Jim, what do you think God wants *you* to do about the mess the church finds itself in?"

This modern-day parable of peacemaking from my dad hit me square between the eyes. I realized we're not called to talk critically about the church or point out its failures; we're called to be part of the solution (even though we can still acknowledge the church's flaws). Our job is to help build up the church, not to be critical of it. Jesus said blessed are the *peacemakers*, not the troublemakers (Matt. 5:9)! So let me ask you the same question my dad asked me: What does God want *you* to do about the mess your church might be in?

> *Our job is to help build up the church, not to be critical of it.*

The Ripple Effect of Obedience

As you consider this question, remember the upside of obedience. Just like rebellion in the church causes ripple effects, so does our obedience to Jesus—but in the opposite way. Humility in the church sphere impacts the other spheres, rippling to the far edges, even to the outer banks of our lives.

The twentieth-century Chinese church leader Watchman Nee helps us understand the importance of the church sphere in relation to the other spheres:

> The Lord calls us to learn obedience in the body, the church, as well as in the home and in the world. Were we to learn well in the body, we would have no difficulty in other areas. The church is where we should begin to learn obedience [to Christ]. It is the place of fulfillment even as it is the place of trial. Should we fail here, we will fail everywhere. If we learn well in the church, the problems of the kingdom, of the world, and of the universe can be solved.[11]

Isn't that encouraging? As humility works itself outward, God's grace reaches even the unknown parts of our lives that need healing, if only we will humble ourselves. Then we might experience what the Lord said to King Solomon: "If my people who are called by my name will humble themselves . . . I will hear from heaven and will forgive their sins and restore their land" (2 Chron. 7:14, NLT). That promise of healing is available to all who are willing to lay down their pride in every area of life and surrender—the blessings of which reverberate throughout our lives and into the world.

Better Understand the Church

The church sphere can be difficult to navigate. That's why we created the "One Another Passages" study, which is a one-time, stand-alone Bible study to help you understand the call to commit to one another, as we laid out in Chapter 9. Embrace this call and disciple others into it as well with this downloadable PDF. Walk through all the "one another" passages in the New Testament to understand better God's heart for the vital role of the church. Download this at TheRevolutionaryDisciple.com/tools.

We also created a worksheet to help you process your ecclesial minimum using Scripture. In Chapter 8, we described what "church" means according to Scripture, but each church must process this issue, especially as our culture changes. The church will continue to face new challenges, so we need to think clearly about which aspects of church life are foundational and which are cultural. This tool will help you process your ecclesial minimum by offering a deeper study of what we outlined in Chapter 8. Process a scriptural definition of church when you download the worksheet "What Is Church?" at TheRevolutionaryDisciple.com/tools.

THE HOME SPHERE

Submit to one another out of reverence for Christ.
— Ephesians 5:21

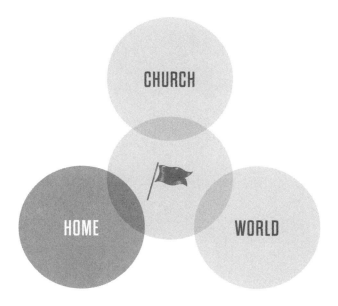

11

WHEN CHURCH BECOMES FAMILY

I (Jim) once took an Uber trip to the airport after I visited my friend Brandon Guindon and the church he pastors in Houston, Texas. Shortly into the ride, I found out my driver was a single mom, and I could see that she loved her son because of his picture she'd hung prominently on the dash of her car.

We had a forty-minute drive, so I began to ask about her son. She told me how she'd gotten pregnant out of wedlock, which had been difficult on her and her family. I asked about her parents and whether they were around to help much.

She told me they were great, but the pregnancy had been hard on their relationship. They were "church-goers," which was why her pregnancy had been difficult for them. I asked why she didn't go to church, and she said it made her feel guilty. Plus, the whole experience had created frustration in her toward her parents' church, which she had attended growing up.

As we continued talking, I realized her highest priority was to discover how to love her son the best she could. She wanted him to get by somehow in this "messed-up world." I affirmed her aspiration, and she opened up even more about her insecurities as a mom.

"I worry about him with all the shootings and stuff. I don't even know what I'm going to do!"

"The first time I saw my kid, I didn't know I could love some-one that much," I said.

"I didn't know that either!" she said, as we connected about how much we love our kids. "But now I'm scared."

I redirected the conversation toward God: "Before we had kids, my wife and I thought our parents were just trying to control us, but now we realize they just knew things we didn't know."

Then she asked a great and humble question: "What advice would you give me about raising a boy as a single mom?"

Without hesitation, I said, "The church." My answer intrigued her, but based on her experience, she didn't see how that would work.

So I told her, "You're a mom and you can do *some things*. But you've got a boy, and he needs to see what a man's life looks like. If a boy doesn't have this, he'll start looking to his peers or to how Hollywood portrays men. But peers aren't men; they're boys. Boys need men, and actors in a movie are not real men to follow.

"If you don't have a husband, you need to have godly men who will help you raise your son, praise him, take him fishing—all those sorts of things. Even though you're a single mom, that doesn't mean you're supposed to do this alone. That's what God's family is for. Plus, the church will show you how to live and give you needed sup-port as you grow!"

I described the difference between attending a church service and truly being part of a church that does life together. I shared about the single moms in my life group and how we get the chance to help them and even invest in their kids. I shared about taking some of their boys hunting and fishing and what that looks like.

She responded, "I've never seen a church like that, where men actually do that, where they actually care about single moms."

"Well, the church you just picked me up at is a church like that," I told her. "They'll teach your kid to fish, and they'll help you when you need help. You need to be around godly families, so your son sees—even though you don't have a husband right now—how a hus-band treats a woman and how a man treats his kids."

"If I go there, do you think they would help me with that?" she asked.

I said yes, and then gave her my friend Brandon's contact information. At this point, our trip to the airport was almost over. I prayed with her as I got out of the car, hoping she would follow my advice. I knew if she tried this parenting thing on her own, her efforts would fall short. Like many others, she needed the church to make it as a single mom.

Soon after, I learned from Brandon that she had followed my advice! She went to Brandon's church the very next week, and within a few months, she joined a home group. I was so happy to hear that because I know being a single parent is so much more difficult without the church.

My answer to her is my answer for all single moms and dads: you need the church because church can become family for you. In addition to my personal experiences, the statistics on single-family homes in the US paint a grim picture. According to the US Census Bureau, a staggering one-third of homes in our country are single-parent households.[1] That's 24.4 million households without two parents at home. That's why we've devoted this entire chapter to the intersection of church and home. With so many single parents today, what are disciples of Christ to do?

The Church Sphere Before the Home Sphere

When we teach the Five Spheres of Discipleship, we intentionally put the church sphere before the family sphere because that's the order in Paul's letter to the Ephesians. I (Jim) often get pushback from people when I tell them the order of the spheres: "Why did Paul put the church sphere before the home sphere? Shouldn't family come first? Is he saying the church is more important than family?" But Paul seems to shift how we think of family in the first place.

When he prays for the church in Ephesus, he says, "I kneel before the Father, from whom *his whole family* in heaven and on earth derives its name" (Eph. 3:14–15). Paul writes about the church family before the biological family, so we try to do the same with the five spheres. Here are three reasons why we believe Paul orders Ephesians this way.

   1. *We receive a new family in Christ.* The church doesn't replace family; *the church becomes our new family.* While this is true for all of us, it's especially important for the many who accept Christ but do not have a biological family. Sometimes, they're single or don't have a believing spouse, so God gives them the church to be their family. Or their biological family walks away from them because of their newfound faith. This includes disciples who convert from their family's religion—from Islam, Hinduism, Buddhism, Mormonism, or New Age, for example—and are abandoned, mistreated, or even persecuted by their families. Some have literally lost their relationships with husbands, wives, sisters, brothers, or even children due to the gospel. So Paul tells those who either have no biological family or their family has turned away from them that the church is their new family. Yet they still hold out hope for unsaved family members.

> *The church becomes our new family.*

   2. *First-generation Christians have to learn discipleship for the first time.* Paul wrote Ephesians to mostly non-Jews who had converted to Christ. These new converts did not have the Old Testament as their foundation for living, so their entire home lives were governed by the teachings of false gods, demonic forces, human tradition, worldly philosophies, and the internal broken compass all people have before Christ redeems us. Like them, we all had an empty way of life without God and without the church. So Paul wrote to help us know the great purpose for which we were saved: "For we are God's workmanship, created in Christ Jesus *to do good works*" (Eph. 2:10). We do good works first in the church, our spiritual family. First-generation Christians need to learn how to be Christlike fathers, mothers, and children from scratch, and the church can help them learn that.

   3. *The church teaches us what family looks like.* In the church, we not only receive sound teaching, which the world doesn't offer, but we also *see disciples model for us* various ways of living: We see what

selfless love looks like, perhaps for the first time. We see what a spiritual father looks like from the lives of spiritual leaders; how spiritual leaders work together rather than against one another; and what a godly marriage looks like. Our kids get to watch other kids live right as children, and we even learn how to relate to our grandparents, cousins, nieces and nephews, aunts and uncles, and parents by our various relationships within the church! Think also about how many men, for example, never learn how to be humble with their wives. Other men in the church can show them how to serve their wife and kids. The church provides a model for those who didn't have a godly example of a father in the home.

Regardless of who we are, the church teaches all of us about all sorts of family relationships, which we can then apply to our home life. We learn how to raise our kids, for example, by our participation in the church. Even if we had Christian parents and learned how to raise kids by watching our parents in a disciple-making home, we can still receive much-needed help in real time from the church. So often others in the church can say to our kids what we've told them before, but our kids listen to them instead of us. Then for all parents, not just single parents, the church can speak into our children's lives to create lasting relational ropes that bind kids together in the faith. In one sense, they can help find salvation for our kids before it's too late.

Every follower of Jesus has a spiritual family, even if their biological family is lacking. Disciples should never have to walk alone because they have the church. So single parents, remember *you need the church*. All other parents, remember *single parents need you to treat them and their kids like family*. Single parents fight the devil too, and he actively accuses singles about their past, holding guilt and shame over their heads. They need the church's acceptance and love. The devil leverages lies about their identity and their past to convince them that they don't belong in the church. He tells them they're not welcome and to go somewhere else. The church must help them reject these lies by treating them like family—because they are. Satan wants them to choose isolation. But families with two parents can help bridge the gaps because that's what family does. We can all seek out these relationships despite our differences—and we're better for it.

The world no longer values the traditional family unit as it once did, and some are even trying to destroy it. Do we downplay the importance of family? Redefine family? Or do away with the traditional family altogether? God has truly revolutionary plans for families and the church if only we will humble ourselves and follow his vision.

This sphere comes back to the four core practices of humility, like all the others: singles and families alike must submit to Christ, serve one another, confess their need for help, and listen to one another's needs. This is such an important topic of conversation that we want to speak directly to singles about it, and then directly to married couples.

A Word to Single Parents

It's important to know that God's plan has always been to "[place] the lonely in families" (Ps. 68:6, NLT), but pride can spoil this. Psalm 68 continues to say that while God places the lonely in families, he also *"makes the rebellious live in a sun-scorched land."* How interesting! What stands in contrast to the lonely? *The rebellious*—who live in a dry, thirsty land (a place of struggle and challenge). Pride distances and isolates all of us, but for single parents, pride leaves them especially vulnerable.

> *Pride distances and isolates all of us.*

Pride turns single parents inward, where they're constantly thinking about themselves. This self-absorbed thinking causes them to feel judged, like everyone's constantly thinking about them and their singleness. They might think, *They all see me as a divorced person and nothing more.* The devil loves to fill in the gaps with these kinds of thoughts and isolate us. Satan whispers into the ears of single parents, *You shouldn't ask for help. You can do it on your own.* Another trick is that he'll take a bad experience you've had with a particular church in the past and taint your view of all of God's people. You start to think, *Church people are all that way! No one will help me; I am too big of a burden. Everyone has too much on their plate—they don't need something else. So I'm not going to mess with that.* This leads to a dark path.

But that doesn't have to be your story. You don't have to let Satan destroy you by separating and isolating you from the church. Single parents can instead reverse the script and humbly ask themselves as they walk into a room, *Who needs my help? How can I serve?* This mentality places your sense of self as a servant instead of the focus of everyone's attention.

Church people often need time and space to figure out how to love single parents too. So single parents, be patient with the church! Get the help and encouragement you need to disciple your kids well.

I (Jim) often use the analogy of an airplane for single parents. If you're on an airplane with a small child, flight attendants always tell you in the case of an emergency, "Put the oxygen mask on yourself first. Then put on your child's mask." If you try to put the mask on your kid first, you'll pass out. And if you pass out, you can't help your kid—and neither of you survives. That's how it is with discipleship for single parents.

We've seen many single parents give up their lives for their kids and not take care of themselves spiritually. But remember, the spheres build on each other. If you don't abide with Christ personally and through your church family, you're going to experience major struggles in the home too. You must learn to walk in Christ before you can successfully disciple your kids at home. If you fall down, get back up and try again! Hopefully, you have the kind of church that lifts the fallen rather than shoots down the wounded. Ask for help, and don't allow your past to keep you from what you really need.

You need relationships within the church from other parents, even if it feels awkward.[2] So go to that small group, push through the Sunday-morning pain of walking into church alone, and constantly ask others for prayer. Then ask others to allow your son or daughter to join them in some kind of event, such as hunting, fishing, or going to a game. Don't be jealous when someone else has experiences with your children. Don't get upset when a mature Christian parent treats your kid like they treat their own by disciplining them—just be thankful for the help. Again, many youth leaders and mature parents have encouraged or corrected our children in ways we couldn't. In these ways, you give people an opportunity to know you and learn how to help you. It takes time for all of us to learn. This is part of humble love, which involves "bearing with one another" (Eph. 4:2). You might have to put up with people who don't "get it," but remember they're also putting up with you! It's all part of the journey, and it's all part of church family relationships.

A Word to Married Couples

Married couples, it's vital that you actively welcome singles into your church life and treat them as equal participants in the body of Christ.[3] This too requires humility. Humility for married couples says, *I will come under God's direction as he places the lonely in families. I will help create a church family that welcomes single parents and others.* This requires us to lay down our desires and serve.

Humility is sensitive to widows, divorcées, and single parents, even to singles who have never been married. If someone has children, treat their kids as your own (with permission and relationship, of course). And disciple single parents' children in some cases, even as you would your own children. When you're in a church group with a majority of married people, make sure the singles in the group feel included. That is, don't act as if singles are any lesser than married people because they don't have a spouse at the group. Many singles say they always feel as though they are the third wheel at church activities. Don't let that happen in your church!

For all married couples, reject the sort of pride that equals self-absorption. This sort of pride says, *I will focus only on my biological family,* or *I will focus only on people who are like me in the same season of life and in the same circumstances.* Instead, embrace the humility that says, *I'm a part of God's family with God as our Father, and we're all family under him.* This is a form of submission. Help a single mom take her child to sports, or dance, or music. And while you're driving them, talk about God, his love given through his commands, and following Jesus. Do for these kids the things you would do for yours. In this way, you serve God's church beautifully. Plus, your household can be an example by displaying humility and love with each other. Your family can serve the church by being role models for others to see and emulate.

Now that we understand how the church and the home spheres relate, we can move on to the full discussion of humility at home. If the church teaches us humility at home, *what exactly* does it teach? And what does a revolutionary family look like? Our answers to these questions carry with them the ability to literally change the world.

12

REVOLUTIONARY FAMILIES

C. S. Lewis reflects on his real-life experience at a pastor's home during lunch one Sunday in *God in the Dock*.[4] The pastor acted much differently at home than at church. At home he spoke to his family in anger, "ruthlessly interrupting" them, yet he had taken plenty of time to preach that very same day about how "the home must be the foundation of our national life."[5]

So Lewis asks us all:

> How, then, *are* people to behave at home? If a man can't
> be comfortable and unguarded, can't take his ease and "be
> himself" in his own house, where can he? That is, I confess, the
> trouble. The answer is an alarming one. There is *nowhere* this
> side of heaven where one can safely lay the reins on the horse's
> neck. It will never be lawful simply to "be ourselves" until
> "ourselves" have become sons of God.[6]

I (Chad) relate to his message here because when I let my guard down, my true self is not always pleasant. Families have the unique ability to reveal our true selves because we can't escape them. This is part of what happened with the conflict with my dad I mentioned in the introduction. I had let my guard down, and in the process, hurt him. This happens in families so easily! That's why Lewis says our homes offer us the opportunity to understand our true selves *and actually be transformed into children of God.*

The home sphere, unlike anywhere else on earth, affords us the opportunity for raw transformation because we can't hide our true selves at home. Yet it's another place where we're called to "lead a life worthy of the calling to which you have been called, *with all humility*" (Eph. 4:1–2, NRSV). As our personal obedience to God grows and we become increasingly humble, it spreads throughout the entire house, making an impact on our spouse and our kids.

This is especially true for fathers. We like what twentieth-century missionary and leadership writer J. Oswald Sanders says: "Humility is the hallmark of the spiritual leader."[7] Because of the way God designed fathers to lead their families, a father's humble attitude and actions uniquely make it much easier for the rest of the family to be humble too. Humble fathers accept their responsibility to lead and realize it's a gift from God to be handled with care.

The home sphere is the most personal one to walk through because it involves our most intimate relationships. At home, we have a great opportunity to grow in humility, but it's often the place of the most tension and strife.

We focus on marriage in this and the next chapter because that relationship shapes the whole family. But we'll also look at the parent-child relationship too. If we will follow Paul's radical instructions in Ephesians, our families can revolutionize our churches, our communities, and the world.

Humility at Home

I (Jim) understand the struggle to be humble at home as a husband and father. Even though I'm a church leader, I still don't have it figured out, and about the time I think I've got something figured out, then I start struggling again! Families are always changing and learning to love each other.

In my marriage, for example, I sometimes struggle to see the need to lay down my life for my wife. When I give in to temptation, I view her as a way to add to my life, not the other way around.

When I take my role as family leader too far, I think to myself, *I'm the spiritual leader. God gives me the authority and the right information, and they need to follow me.* Even writing that, I realize how self-focused and prideful those thoughts are. During my thirty-plus years of marriage, I've learned to recognize what a humble husband should think about marriage: *We are a partnership, and God speaks to my wife as a vital part of the partnership. I don't make plans on my own—we make plans together.*

Humility reminds me that my job is not to make decisions by myself and be the commander-in-chief of the home. That's pride. Instead, my job is to lead by facilitating decisions. God desires for leaders to lead by example and service, rather than by pounding their fist about what others should be doing. I need to do what Jesus, our great example, did when he gave himself up for his bride, the church. That's the humility of Christ in action. Good spiritual leaders know the right thing to do, and they act. If they don't know the right thing to do, they lead a search to find the right thing. They lead prayer time to discover the Lord's will; they facilitate discussion; and they open the door for receiving wise counsel from other believers who are mature.

Similar to the struggles I have as a husband, my wife has struggled to submit to my leadership because she sometimes struggles to trust others in general. Her struggle sometimes surfaces because I have hurt her, but we can all struggle with trust because we've all been hurt by others.

We must forgive one another, and forgiveness requires humility.

If we want to be in relationship with people—especially family—we *will* experience pain. So we must forgive one another, and forgiveness requires humility. But God calls all of us to give our pain to him, to let go of our past, and to step into the present, which involves the risk of being hurt again. Yet where risk exists, there is also potential reward. That's why Paul spent so much space in Ephesians giving us instructions about family relationships. He knew that even though all families are broken to different degrees— remember they had divorce back then too—the family unit is a vital place for making disciples.

Consider what humility looks like at home. When we're children, a humble attitude leads us to submit to our parents' guidance. When we're adults, humility helps us serve our families, submit to our spouse, listen to input, and confess our mistakes along the way. We never graduate from the four core practices of humility! We know that marriage is about serving each other, listening to each other, and confessing our weaknesses to each other. But we often downplay the importance of submitting to one another.

Let's look at Ephesians 5:21–6:4, where humility is at the center of Paul's instructions: He says, "Submit to one another out of reverence for Christ," which he applies first to the husband-wife relationship (Eph. 5:21). "Out of reverence for Christ" reminds us that only when we're connected to Christ and submissive to him can we submit to other people.

Submitting to One Another

Because the roles of the sexes in the family can be such a controversial topic, we want to put our cards on the table at the beginning. Both of us believe, as the Scriptures reveal and historic faith repeats, the biblical family unit is formed only by the marriage of a man and a woman. We see marriage as a commitment men and women make before God to one another that lasts until Jesus returns or death takes them home. In our view, each sex has equal value and importance but unique roles in the family.

Scripture emphasizes both the equal value and privilege we all have in Christ for salvation (Gal. 3:28–29) as well as the differences between men and women in family life (Eph. 5:21–33). Even through cultural progress, human nature remains the same. Wives and mothers have unique roles, equally valuable to the unique roles of husbands and fathers. Together, men and women complement one another. But society today attacks the family. Part of today's rebellion in North American society and beyond is due to a rejection of the God-instituted roles of men and women.[8]

Ephesians 5:21–27 provides a great introduction to how men and women can submit to each other. Paul writes:

> Submit to one another out of reverence for Christ. Wives, submit to your husbands as to the Lord. For the husband is the head of the wife as Christ is the head of the church, his body, of which he is the Savior. Now as the church submits to Christ, so also wives should submit to their husbands in everything. Husbands, love your wives, just as Christ loved the church and gave himself up for her to make her holy, cleansing her by the washing with water through the word, and to present her to himself as a radiant church, without stain or wrinkle or any other blemish, but holy and blameless.

Did you notice how *both husbands* and *wives* are to submit to each other? I (Chad) find helpful the nuance of the word "submit" here. It means to "come under" one another, and it's sometimes used as a military term for coming under someone's leadership. The same word is used for the authority that the Father gave to the Son by placing everything "under his feet" (Eph. 1:22). We're all ultimately called to submit to Christ's authority, but in the home, there's a sense to which we all *come under* each other in different ways. While submission takes different forms, we should all submit to one another. Both men and women should submit to each other: husbands submit to their wives by loving them as Christ loves the church (5:25), and wives submit to their husbands by respectfully deferring to them (5:24, 33).

The Revolutionary Marriage

Submitting to our spouse to love and respect them enacts humility and flies in the face of the "curses" humanity received in Genesis 3.

Adam and Eve faced the consequences of their rebellion toward God when the serpent convinced them to put their self-interest above God's will. Remember how it happened?

First, the serpent turned man and woman against one another. Adam, rather than leading and protecting Eve, stood by and allowed the devil to tempt her. He watched her try the fruit first, then he ate it too. By eating it, Adam further rebelled against God. God confronted Adam, who, in turn, blamed Eve (Gen. 3:6–12).

This progression shows that from these earliest moments of human history, husbands and wives were already pitted against each other by their own pride! No wonder the spousal relationship remains that way under the curse. God said to the woman, "Your desire will be for your husband, and he will rule over you" (Gen. 3:16). The Hebrew word commonly translated "desire" here relates to a wife's desire for power over the husband (not sexual desire for him). That is, a woman's strong desire in marriage would be to control her husband and manipulate him *toward her desired outcome.*

So unredeemed, a wife's major struggle toward her husband is about power and control dynamics. Similarly, a husband's temptation is to "rule over" his wife in an authoritarian way. These desires come from pride, which pits us against one another and destroys marriages left and right. But a restored marriage relationship in Christ comes about by humility through mutual submission.

In Christ, *we come under* one another, and reverse the curse. Wives are to submit to their husbands by showing respect to them, and husbands are to submit to their wives by serving them. Each action helps husbands and wives *come under* the other. How does this work? We have to learn the humility of Christ—*from Christ*—to reverse the curse. This is a tall order for both husbands and wives.

The challenge of this comes because worldly cultures—including progressive Christian cultures—teach us differently. They skew roles in the home or teach no roles at all. While these teachings might seem alluring, they encourage people to feed their desire over God's plan. Just as the enemy of our souls sought to fan the flames of pride in the Garden of Eden, so today the enemy seeks to lure us into rejecting God's design—in the home and beyond. Sin teaches couples to fight for their individual rights and preferences, but Christ teaches couples to love one another through submission and service. That's a revolutionary marriage.

The world doesn't understand this because it has rejected the gospel of Christ and, as a result, lives an unsatisfying life in darkness and confusion. So as we embrace the revolutionary ways of Jesus, we also reject the ways of the world. The world tempts us to argue with God's design, rather than to embrace it humbly. What does humility actually look like at home? With this foundation from Ephesians, let's look at the more practical side of humility in the home, not just between husbands and wives but also between parents and children.

> *Christ teaches couples to love one another through submission and service.*

13

WALKING HUMBLY WITH YOUR SPOUSE

I (Chad) have been married for only five years, so I'm a novice at marriage. As a result, I have a good number of examples of what humility *does not look like!* Let me share just one.

Early in our relationship, while we were dating, I learned my wife appreciates acts of service. Remembering this, I surprised her one day and quietly unloaded the dishwasher and cleaned the whole kitchen before she had the chance. *Good work, me!* I thought to myself.

Well, a whole day went by, and she didn't comment on my act of service. So I started to wonder if she'd even noticed. A week went by—still no recognition. Then came the moment of my great disappointment. We were in the kitchen together, and she said, "I'd like you to help out more around the house." *What?* I thought. *Had she not realized what I had just done last week?*

Instead of receiving her words with humility, however, I stupidly opened my mouth and explained how sacrificial I had been the week before. Then I flat out said, "I deserve more credit." Yeah, big mistake. Immediately, I regretted it. I had tried to get credit for something that was really just my normal duty as a husband—serving my wife. Plus, my wife had cleaned the kitchen many times, and I hadn't thanked her at all. When I realized my error, I tried to learn from my mistake and grow in humility.

So I made another attempt to be humble through service and simply cleaned the kitchen when it wasn't expected, not seeking any credit. Sure enough when I did it—this time with a better motive—she recognized my service to her! She thanked me, and we both moved on. That was it. I had humbly listened to her and served. Nothing fancy, just the simple service of disciples of Jesus.

The Heart of a Servant

Like Jesus taught in Luke 17:10, we should say after we've served someone, "We are unworthy servants; we have only done our duty." This type of humility stands in contrast with those outside of Christ. Of course, serving others is not unique to those in Christ, so what makes Christlike humility different? We do what we do "out of reverence for Christ," not only because of what he's done for us but also because God asks us to "serve wholeheartedly" out of love (Eph. 5:21; 6:7).

As my story shows, we can easily slip into pride at home, even with something as simple as cleaning the kitchen. Humility looks pretty normal and doesn't draw attention to itself. Pride, on the other hand, aims to get something in return (recognition, credit, or applause). Bottom line: a humble spouse serves simply for the sake of the other person, no strings attached. This is part of what Paul's getting at in Ephesians 5 as he lays out what husbands, especially, are expected to do for their wives.

Real humility means we admit our failings.

As we discussed in the last chapter, Paul instructs men and women to submit to one another, and this reveals how God orders the home for those in Christ. Yet we all fall short of this. Real humility means we admit our failings, rather than get defensive about our blunders. We don't justify ourselves but humbly admit our selfishness. We ask forgiveness along the way and continue to seek growth. Even the proverbs acknowledge this: "The godly may trip seven times, but they will get up again" (Prov. 24:16, NLT). We always get up and try again.

What Humility Looks Like in a Marriage

We invite you to learn from our mistakes (and any successes the Lord has given us), as we share with you about growing in humility at home.

Husbands, love your wives by serving. I (Jim) have struggled to learn how to truly love my wife by serving her. My wife, Lori, and I come from completely different backgrounds, and the mix of our personality traits, filters, and families of origin does not make for an easily harmonious relationship. Our styles of life and working together as a couple are as far as the east is from the west. Some marriages are not like ours, though, and it's easier for them to relate to one another. But since we come from such different backgrounds, our differences have challenged me to learn how to love her (and I'm still learning).

As one example, when my parents and siblings got together growing up, we were loud. Well, we tend to be the same way even today. Everyone talks over each other, and if you want to be heard, you have to speak loudly. To us, talking loudly isn't rude, just our way of relating. Not so with Lori's family. They were quiet growing up, and if you ever raised your voice, you were really mad about something. So Lori and I had to work this out. Our conversations would go something like this:

After I would get animated and loud, she would say, "Quit yelling at me."

"I'm not yelling at you."

"Yes, you are!"

Realizing that was simply how I had learned to relate growing up in my household was hard for Lori. I struggled to relate to her.

In the early years of our marriage, Lori struggled relating to me too, because when Lori would get mad, she'd find a quiet way to say the meanest, most awful things that my family would never say in a million years. Was my family loud? Yes. Mean? No. But to her, loud and mean were the same thing.

We went to a counselor to get help, and to my surprise, the counselor focused *on my part, not hers!* He said, "Jim, to love is to understand your wife. If for Lori yelling includes speaking loudly, and you speak loudly anyway, then you're not loving her. Whether or not it's yelling in your eyes doesn't matter. The question is this: Are you showing love to her? Biblical love gives what the other needs, rather than what you want to give."

His words just drilled me. It was hard for me to embrace the fact that I had not been loving my wife as I ought. Certain channels of relating had been common for me since my childhood. They were like rails of a train track that had to be reconfigured in my brain. It was one thing for me to *realize* something like this. It was another thing to *actually change* a certain way I had been relating to others my entire life. Getting animated and raising my voice had never been wrong for me until I was married to Lori. But now I knew it was wrong and unloving in our marriage.

By the grace of God, I began making strides. For Lori, just that I admitted I was wrong and tried to change was a big deal, because for so long she had felt helpless that I wouldn't even consider my actions wrong. Thank God that Lori is a grace-giver.

As I was beginning to change during that time but fell back into old ways, she would say, "Wow, I haven't seen that guy in a while. Are you okay?" I'm so glad for that because she was walking with Jesus and giving what Jesus gives—continued grace. Quite honestly, if it wasn't for the help of a counselor, an ongoing abiding relationship with Jesus, and good friends who hold me accountable, I would not have the good marriage I have today.

Husbands, our job is to love our wives and to lay down our lives for them in an understanding way. This listening and understanding piece is huge, and it comes from Scripture! A parallel to

Ephesians 5:25 is 1 Peter 3:7, where men are literally called to "live with [our] wives in an understanding way" (ESV). God inspired Peter to help husbands learn to navigate life in the home with their wives by taking on a personal understanding of how their wives need to be loved. Peter adds, "So that nothing will hinder your prayers" (v. 7). Let that sink in. How a husband treats his wife directly affects his personal relationship with God.

I (Jim) see this in the way my relationship with my wife affects my relationship with my father-in-law, Frank. How could I mistreat Frank's daughter but have a good relationship with Frank? I'd have another thing coming! In the same way, my wife's heavenly Father is not okay with me treating his daughter poorly. If I think I can have a great time with the Lord in prayer but not try to care for Lori, I will have a real problem with the Lord.

Where does humility fit into this passage? The very next verse in 1 Peter 3 brings us back to humility: "Finally, all of you, live in harmony with one another; be sympathetic, love as brothers, be compassionate and *humble*" (v. 8). Husbands have a unique obligation to live humbly by understanding their wives. Husbands lead in the home by *initiating* love through service, as Christ *initiated* loving the church by laying down his life for her.

Wives, respect your husbands by submitting. Women can just as easily struggle to live out this passage of mutual submission from Ephesians 5:21–33. The issue, as we mentioned, is controversial in our culture today. Part of the reason for this is because we don't understand biblical authority and submission in general.

> Our value comes from our identity as children of God.

We think equal value means equal authority and roles, but that's just not how it works. Our value as people does not come from anything *we do*, anyway! Our value comes from our identity as children of God, which comes through our relationship with Christ. The struggle, then, can be resolved by reorienting ourselves to our identity before God. Why do we need to have a certain role that might be perceived as more valuable than other roles? Culture tries to hijack how we view family roles, but disciples of Jesus must look to Scripture for how to live—and Scripture teaches equal value and unique roles.

Paul calls women to submit to their husbands: "Wives, submit to your husbands as to the Lord" (Eph. 5:22). What does this look like? It's a dance. As the husband leads, so the wife follows. While leadership covers many aspects of life, it primarily has to do with holiness and love. The husband seeks to lead his family spiritually, and the wife follows. A husband wants to get involved in a home group, for example, so the wife follows; a husband decides to serve the poor, so the wife follows; a husband decides to have family Bible study every morning, so the wife follows. In this way, the wife allows her husband to lead the family spiritually. Wives can surely initiate these things too, but she defers to her husband's leadership in the process.

A humble wife treats her husband with respect instead of disdain (Eph. 5:33). She allows him the driver's seat and encourages him, instead of taking the wheel when he appears to have lost the way. The greatest temptation for a wife here is to try to take over the leadership role when she doesn't agree with his direction. We cannot control our spouses; we can only control our humble posture toward them. A humble wife submits to her husband's leadership. Here's the key: even if your husband's not a perfect leader, you're still called to follow him "as to the Lord." That's difficult because he's surely not going to be perfect like the Lord. Yet this is how God ordered the home sphere, and even if we don't like it, we follow God's will, not ours.

A final word to husbands. Humble leadership is not about calling all the shots but leading the way toward serving together. A good leader in the home facilitates discussions, cultivates the partnership between husband and wife, and shares in the work at hand. A humble husband listens more than he speaks. Why? Because God often speaks to husbands *through their wives* to receive the right counsel and direction. If we're not careful, our leadership becomes a

> A humble husband listens more than he speaks.

dictatorship. This happens when a husband stops listening to and caring for his wife's vital role in his life as a leader. Leadership at home becomes holy when both husband and wife work humbly together as one.

In the home, everyone has different roles. We each have a piece of humble pie to eat—different flavors for each of us. We see this throughout Scripture, and if we are going to follow Jesus as husbands and wives, we must embrace the authority structure God gives us in Ephesians. In the home, no role is above any other role. Jesus reminds us that in him, the world's hierarchy is flipped: "The greatest among you will be your servant. For whoever exalts himself will be humbled, and whoever humbles himself will be exalted" (Matt. 23:11–12).

Fostering Trust in Marriage

Our wives and others have told us that a great challenge for women comes down to trust. Women are called to submit to and show respect toward their husbands, but if women struggle to trust men because of previous abuses of male power, men can build trust by serving God above all else. Her trust can grow as she sees her husband put this sort of God-centered service into practice.

Stephen M. R. Covey talks about the importance of building trust in his book *The Speed of Trust*. He says trust:

> Undergirds and affects the quality of every relationship, every communication, every work project, every business venture, every effort in which we are engaged. It changes the quality of every present moment and alters the trajectory and outcome of every future moment of our lives—both personally and professionally.[9]

Trust is the foundation for any relationship, so fostering trust in your marriage is vital. So what does it look like to build trust? It looks like a husband regularly asking his wife's perspective, formulating plans with her, and not only praying for God's will with his wife but also implementing family plans together. Wives learn to trust husbands when husbands lead the way and protect their little flock along the road of life. Trust for disciples is a choice we make out of reverence for Christ.

We hold reverence for Christ because Christ is the head of the church (Eph. 5:23). God created an authority structure in the home, and that authority comes from God through the husband. This is how God has chosen to disseminate authority in the home sphere. Just as he designed different roles within the church, so he arranged different roles for the home: "God has arranged the parts in the body, every one of them, just as he wanted them to be" (1 Cor. 12:18). It's God's arrangement, not ours. Husbands don't get "more power." They get a different level of accountability, pressure, and responsibility to lead their household as servants.

Marriage as a Partnership

Another reason we, especially Americans, struggle with a biblical view of marriage—where we each have equal value and unique roles—is that we've lost sight of *the goal of marriage*. As Gary Thomas writes in *Sacred Marriage*, marriage is "a call to holiness more than happiness."[10]

This issue relates to our understanding of the gospel. Many of us have believed in an "American gospel," as Bill Hull and Brandon Cook call it in *The False Promise of Discipleship*. The American gospel says *God exists for me*: he fulfills my goals, my desires, and my dreams. But this is based on a false gospel that is both self-focused and inaccurate. While our individual desires have a place in God's heart, God's goal for marriage and our lives is to fulfill *his vision*, not ours. The true gospel of God's kingdom is good for us, but it's not about us at the core. So we can think of marriage like a partnership in the kingdom—a means by which to fulfill God's calling in our lives.

Based on our experiences in our own marriages, as well as working with couples in ministry, we offer three practical pieces of advice for both husbands and wives to cultivate a truly humble, king-dom-focused partnership.

1. Give without condition. As we mentioned, some of our troubles in marriage come from a false view of the purpose of marriage. But even when we know God's kingdom purpose for marriage, we must continue learning how to treat our spouse as a partner toward God's calling throughout the rest of our lives. Yes, submitting to a husband is much easier, for example, when he's submitting to God's plan. But what happens when he's being selfish? Do wives still submit then? Author Emerson Eggerichs points out the importance of "unconditional respect," as he calls it, in his watershed marriage book, *Love and Respect.*[11] We as Christians are used to hearing about unconditional love, but what about unconditional *respect*?

The premise of Eggerichs's book is based on Ephesians 5:33: that God has called husbands specifically to love their wives and wives specifically to respect their husbands. Both happen by choice rather than a feeling or an opinion of whether or not the other person deserves it. When one partner chooses not to give love or not to respect unconditionally, our marriages get on what Eggerichs calls "the crazy cycle." This is where the husband's lack of love triggers his wife's disrespect of him. Couples also get caught in this cycle when the wife's disrespect triggers her husband to neglect loving her like he should.

What keeps us from spiraling to this point? Giving unconditional love and unconditional respect. This last piece is unique, and we've found it to be important for couples. Bottom line: Why would we love unconditionally but not also respect without condition? Both actions go both ways. Husbands should not just love through service but also show respect, and wives should not just respect but also love their husbands through service.[12] Paul simply names the difficult-to-do actions for each partner in Ephesians 5. If we always have spoken (or unspoken) conditions that our spouse must meet for us to treat them properly, we'll stay in "the crazy cycle." But unconditional love and unconditional respect break the cycle of jostling for position and rights. They counteract pride and foster humility.

Talking about unconditional respect might seem like an oxymoron because we always talk about how people must "earn respect." But earning respect doesn't make sense in the economy of God's grace, just like earning love doesn't make sense. We don't expect our spouse to earn our love, do we? So why must husbands earn the respect of their wives? In Christ, there's no earning, only giving. And both partners are called to give both love and respect to the other without condition because we're a team. If there's always a condition, then the team will repeatedly break down. We've got a higher calling toward our spouse than that, so let's walk in it!

2. Call another couple for help. The most practical piece of advice I (Chad) got about marriage was to find an older couple to call when we couldn't find resolution to a conflict. This is especially important when we get caught in "the crazy cycle." The idea is to ask an older couple we trust to be available for those standstill moments of "intense fellowship." This means we can use our phone-a-friend card when we don't agree about who's right and who's wrong.

This advice sounded hard at first, and it took an entire two years of marriage before I mustered up the courage to ask an older couple if we could call them when we got stuck. Even then, picking up the phone and making the call was difficult. My pride got in the way, and I was too proud to admit we needed help. But when we opened up this reservoir of God's grace, it was a great leveling ground for our marriage relationship. Talk about discipleship for couples! To ask a more experienced couple to talk through a real-life issue with you as a couple takes humility.

I (Jim) can tell you that this isn't just advice for younger couples—all couples need others to help them out, even for those who think they're marriage veterans! As with the rest of life, when we humble ourselves in marriage to get help, God lifts us up and brings life into our marriages.

3. Make plans together. While husbands are called to lead their families, one way we can love our wives is by inviting them into our responsibilities. Instead of acting like a lone ranger, we can invite our spouses not just to join us in the implementation of a plan but also in the creation of a plan. Husbands, ask yourself, *Do I truly see and understand my wife's perspective when we're making decisions? Do I truly believe God gave my wife to me with a unique perspective and wisdom that I don't have on my own?*

I (Jim) have seen many a husband come up with a plan on his own, and then tell his wife, "Okay, let's implement this plan I came up with!" But she didn't have any part in its creation, so why would she buy in? The job of a leader in the family is to facilitate finding the solution to a problem, not to figure it out all on their own.

So again, husbands, let your wives into your processes. That's part of being a humble leader. And don't just pay lip service to this, either. Really listen, understand, and weigh what she says. Humble spouses and good marriage partners listen to each other, make plans together, and submit to one another—as they both humble themselves "under God's mighty hand" (1 Pet. 5:6).

Paul begins the home life—what we're calling Sphere 3—with the marriage relationship in Ephesians 5:21–33, then he moves on to the parent-child relationship in Ephesians 6:1–4. So let's turn to the parent-child relationship to expand our understanding of walking humbly in the home sphere.

14

HUMBLE PARENTING

In AD 9, the temple in Jerusalem bustled with hundreds of thousands of people for the Feast of Passover. Among the people walked the boy Jesus. Without his parents' knowledge, Jesus had stayed in Jerusalem, talking with teachers at the temple, while his parents journeyed to their home in Nazareth.

His parents searched for Jesus for three days. When they found him, Mary said, "Son, why have you treated us like this? Your father and I have been anxiously searching for you" (Luke 2:48). At first blush, this doesn't sound like Jesus honored and submitted to his parents, does it? But Jesus' response to his mother and his subsequent actions reveal his humility: "Why were you searching? . . . Didn't you know I had to be in my Father's house?" (v. 49). Jesus was ultimately submissive to his heavenly Father. Yet he still submitted to his earthly parents: "He went down with them and came to Nazareth *and was submissive to them*" (v. 51, ESV).

Notice the progression of Jesus' movement: he *went down* to Nazareth and *was submissive to* his parents. He was God's Messiah even then, yet he submitted to his earthly parents in obedience.[13] Jesus knew who he was before God and chose to go lower by submitting. We see how Jesus

> *Jesus knew who he was and chose to go lower.*

exemplified humility even at home. But this reveals something else to us: God delegates authority to parents. This means God gives us great responsibility to disciple our kids. But we have a major challenge to work through as parents: our pride.

Two Forms of Pride in a Parent

In our experience, pride, more than anything else, keeps parents from making disciples at home. This shows itself by parents who either become passive or authoritarian. Both of these reveal pride and foil the process of discipleship at home.

Passive parents. Parents who struggle with a certain kind of pride believe the lie that says, "My kids are exceptional; they will turn out fine, even if I don't do the work." When they believe this, they reject their God-given authority in the home to disciple their kids. I (Jim) hear so many parents say, "I don't want to press my views on my kids," or "I want to let them grow up to make their own decision." Comments like these sound right, according to the world we live in, but they're rooted in a parent's desire to be their child's buddy.

Yet the goal of a parent is not to be their kid's buddy but to be a godly, wise leader who trains their child for a life of faithfulness. We hope to become friends with our kids, but that isn't how it starts. Scripture tells us that all children need correction: "Folly is bound up in the heart of a child, but the rod of discipline will drive it far from him" (Prov. 22:15). We live in a world that rejects human sinfulness and says children will become a blessing if we just leave them to themselves. This isn't biblical, and it's one of the reasons for the state of our fallen world.

Perhaps you lean toward passivity in parenting because you were never discipled in the home, or you grew up with an authoritarian parent whose version of faith pushed you away. Your temptation will be to live in fear of being an overbearing parent. You'll be tempted to treat your kids like a friend and only give them suggestions and advice. Humility for you starts with embracing your God-given authority—which is part of knowing who you are before God.

Remember our definition? A humble disciple doesn't believe they're better than they are; they know exactly who they are—nothing more and nothing less.

Authoritarian parents. These parents, on the other hand, misuse their authority. Of course, there's a difference between authoritarianism and *being authoritative.* Authoritative parents rightly embrace God-given authority (or "power") and its purpose. That's good. But *authoritarian* parents misuse their God-given power to coerce, manipulate, or make their children unnecessarily angry.

Parents like this—when they're not seeking God's purpose for them—want their kids to make their life as a parent easy. Perhaps they simply don't want their kids to embarrass them, or they want their kids to meet their own needs. Authoritarian parents can even intend the best for their children, but the way they seek to disciple their kids comes out wrong. It might come out in anger or in fear, which drives their kids away from them—and from the Lord. Parents like this have received their authority from God, but they've taken it too far by discarding the goal of parenting, which is teaching our kids how to love God and people relationally.

Both passive and authoritarian parents operate out of pride. As hard as it is to admit, prideful parents seek to serve themselves above their kids. Both of us have done this, so we understand the challenge! If you see either of these approaches in yourself at all, take heart: God can do a new work in you and in your children. By the power of the Spirit, you can learn to walk with humility at home. Christ offers hope for all of us, no matter where we might be in our parenting walk. Remember, it's a journey. We can experience a course correction at any point, especially when we allow time, community, and humility into our lives!

Say Yes to Discipleship at Home

We pursue humble parenting by first knowing our rightful place as authority figures for our children. Navigating this is an art that we learn as our children get older. Then the older our children get, the more we lead by giving suggestions and advice rather than directives. For small children, though, parents cannot simply speak wisdom and expect to convince their child through logic—we must discipline them.[14] All parents have the great opportunity to model humility in the home, but working this out practically can be difficult to navigate. So what practical ways can we train our children to learn humble love from Jesus so they can be saved from—as hard as it feels to say—their own pride and selfishness? How can we model humility as parents in ways that teach them to walk humbly too?

First, if you're already trying to disciple your kids, huge props for simply trying! You're already heading in the right direction because few parents intentionally disciple their kids. If you feel like you don't know what to do, then welcome to the club! You will not do it perfectly, but if you set your mind on the goal—to teach your kids to love God with all their heart, mind, body, and strength, and people too—you're on the right track. Throughout Scripture, we're commanded to raise our children to know the Lord. Of course, our children will have to decide for themselves whether or not they will accept those teachings. We must teach the real Jesus, so our kids can make an informed decision either to follow or reject him.

I (Chad) have many friends who grew up in the church but have now left the faith entirely. I'm convinced that those in my generation (millennials) and in younger generations leave the faith for a good reason—because often they reject a false Jesus. Some leave for other reasons, but many leave because they were not properly discipled to understand scriptural Christianity. They had believed a watered-down gospel they picked up from various sources and ended up rejecting it. In the end, they rejected a god of the culture, not the God of the Gospels.

We must teach our children the truth about the real Jesus and the real gospel in Scripture. This is not the church's job, the children's minister's job, or the youth minister's job. This is the job of parents. God gave us the authority and responsibility to do this. I know this from Scripture, and I'm only beginning to learn what this looks like with my young kids at home! Humble parents accept their responsibility and lead courageously by discipling their kids. This takes humility on our part because we have to admit when we don't know what to do. We confess our mistakes, and we ask for help from others. Saying yes to discipling our kids is a must, but it takes courage to step out in faith and humbly learn through trial and error.

If you haven't yet decided to disciple your kids, don't be afraid to say yes. God set up the church so you can have wise counsel. You were not intended to parent alone. Once you've made the decision to disciple your kids and you get in the game—that's half the battle. Then the challenge becomes figuring out the details of what the rest looks like. For clearly right or wrong issues, that's one thing. But what about all the muddy issues of life? Where do you turn in moments like that? The temptation of pride is to go it alone, but humble parents confess that they don't have all the answers and seek wise counsel.

Seeking Wise Counsel in Parenting

I (Jim) have seen so many first-generation Christians in our church who have humbled themselves and decided raising their kids was too important just to wing it. They began to seek help by watching others, asking questions, and learning as they went. Thankfully, many older Christians at our church shared their successes and failures with them. Even when we think we know the answer but we're not sure, just admitting that takes humility. It's like when my friend Darin's sixteen-year-old daughter, Jayci, wanted a Bible verse tattoo. Darin is on staff at Real Life, so I got a front-row view as this all unfolded.

This was a tough spot for Darin and his wife. They are both first-generation Christians, and Darin wasn't sure what to do with his emerging teenage girl who was seeking her own direction for the first time. Christians today have different ways of understanding what's right or wrong on this issue, and faithful disciples land on both sides of the fence. Darin didn't want his daughter to get the tattoo, but he knew the bigger picture of what was at stake—his daughter's heart and his relationship with her. So he asked me for advice.

First, a little background on my relationship with Darin. He has watched my successes and failures as a father and husband over the years because I have openly shared my life with him. He and his wife wanted to say no to Jayci, but they didn't know how to handle the situation without coming across as overbearing or legalistic. Because they had seen Lori and I wrestle through decisions, Darin felt comfortable saying to his wife, "Let's go ask Jim."

When Darin asked my advice, I told him, "When I was younger, I fought with my kids on many of the wrong battlefields about things that weren't that important, which led to tension. Then when I had to stand on an issue that actually was important, it seemed to my kids like I always made every issue too important."

I told Darin that hair and tattoos are not as important as many other things at this stage. "I'd let your daughter get the tattoo," I told him. "Here's the deal, though: I wouldn't pay for it, and I would let her know your concerns about it." I told him this is not a black-and-white issue, and there will be many more important ones later. If our kids see our humility in our willingness to seek wise counsel, then the process will truly impact them.

Darin showed humility first by confessing to his wife that he didn't know, and second by listening to advice from someone else (two of the core practices of humility). He modeled a humble heart. Darin and his wife then prayed about what to do together and chose a path. They gave their daughter an opportunity to see their heart.

After all of this, Darin told Jayci, "I talked about this with Jim and got some wise counsel, and I'm going to let you do it."

She was happy to get the tattoo, but even more, she was impacted by seeing how much her father cared about her heart and got wise counsel. She also saw how Christianity isn't just about the rules, and that some issues don't have clear answers. When I saw her the next Sunday, I talked to her and made sure she recognized her dad's humility in how he had handled the situation.

This story was a win because Darin led his family with humility; I, as a part of the church, was now seen by his daughter as one who is for her; and now, with a clear example of advice-asking, perhaps later she will allow other voices to speak into her life about things that matter more than a tattoo.

Plus, Darin caught the vision for how to gain trust and disciple his daughter at the heart level by seeking wise counsel. He knew that by letting his daughter have a place to be herself, and perhaps make mistakes, he could cultivate a relationship with her. That's part of being a humble disciple maker as a parent: being vulnerable and making space for the other person—where they are actually at, not where the parent thinks they should be.

Humility says, "I don't have to be right all the time, and when I am wrong, I will say that I'm sorry." Humble people seek wise counsel, rather than coming to the proud place that acts like a know-it-all. This type of church-family interaction that Darin and I were able to model for his family shows what humility looks like *in relationship*, as we've mentioned. When we model this, God makes us become humble parents who seek advice from others in the church.[15]

Humbly Parenting at the Heart Level

One of the keys to humble, relational discipleship in the home is to disciple our kids at the heart level. Paul instructs parents, "Do not exasperate your children" (Eph. 6:4). A parent "exasperates" their child when they cause unnecessary anger by constantly picking at them, which frustrates and discourages them. It comes from harsh, misplaced, or misdirected discipline. *It comes from pride in a parent.* Our kids start to see us as judgmental, which influences how they see God. This is harmful, and it never makes us happy as parents.

Heart-level discipleship, on the other hand, helps guard against these mistakes. As my dad and I (Chad) wrote about in *Dedicated*, heart-level discipleship means we lead with relationship rather than just rules.[16] By respecting a child's will and allowing them grace to learn obedience over time, we follow Paul's command not to make our children unnecessarily angry. Excessive or coercive discipline leads to exasperation. So discipline your children through loving relationship and reasonable rules. When you see your anger take control, back off and ask for God's help—at the heart level! When you fail, tell your kids you love them and confess you're sorry for your part, even if your child was wrong for their part. If we as parents are only 10 percent wrong, we are still 100 percent wrong for our part. No one can make us act like fools. It's our sin, and we must own that.

Paul continues, "Instead, bring them up in the training and instruction of the Lord" (Eph. 6:4). With this, he offers an alternative to exasperation, which is "training and instruction." God clearly wants parents to help their children to learn obedience. The two words here for discipline both involve discipleship toward maturity, but their differences are important: training our kids is teaching them what *to do*; instructing them is teaching them what *not to do*.

Our kids need both guidance (what to do) and correction (what not to do). Together, training and instruction form a child's heart. Knowing these positive and negative sides of discipling our kids helps us guide them into mature adulthood.

I (Jim) have learned that as our children grow up, we can move from more of a command style of parenting to dealing more directly with them at the heart level. When they're young, they don't have the capacity to understand "the why" as much. But as they grow, we can teach our kids practical life lessons and explain the reasoning behind our rules more often. That's how we can guide their hearts. To get there, though, we must come in humbly and with patience, instead of impatiently saying, "Because I told you so." Celebrate what you value in them as much as you correct or instruct them.

As they get older, start discipling them at the heart level *by sharing your heart* about life issues as they come up. If you don't share your heart, they'll never open up and be honest about what's going on *in their hearts*. Humbly share your own failures. So many parents are not willing to share like this because they think they're giving their child permission to sin. But it doesn't have to be that way.

You can share your story of sin as a parent in a way that doesn't give license to but warns against sin. As you honestly share past and current failures with your kids and affirm how much you love them, you'll be able to communicate that warning and how you don't want them to get hurt or to hurt others.

I (Chad) remember how my parents confessed to mistakes while I was growing up. This has always been a gift to me, but it's especially helpful now that I have a family of my own. Whenever my parents made a mistake, they'd openly confess to the whole family. It sounds weird, but it was normal in our family culture. As a result, now I know what it looks like to confess my wrongs with my kids. I learned humility by watching it in action. Now it's a part of my family's culture too.

Further, as we listen to our children, we learn *what they're feeling*. But remember to open up first because you might not find out *why they feel the way they do* unless you share your heart first. Share your heart by telling them where you have been and where you are now in your own walk with Christ. Tell them how you're really doing and how God is convicting you. Practices like these offer the best way to help them start evaluating their hearts too.

Remember, discipleship in the home sphere comes back to teaching our kids how to love and be loved. Our goal as parents is to cultivate a loving relationship with our kids so they'll be formed from the inside out. You've probably heard that "more is caught than taught." This truth is more obvious in the home than in any other sphere of discipleship! How you *model* humble love is much more impactful than what you *teach about* humble love.

> *How you model humble love is much more impactful than what you teach.*

So you should both model and intentionally teach them the ways of God from Scripture. You can tell your kids all you want about what love should be like, but if you teach them *and show them* the love of Christ through humble service, submission, listening, and confession, you will give them the greatest possible opportunity to "catch it" from you. So spend time with them to truly know them, and engage in real, meaningful dialogue with them about the things of God. Become a student of your children to truly disciple them at the heart level. It's worth the extra effort.

Passing the Torch

Be humble in your home by developing a loving and transformative relationship with your kids—even when they leave home. Then you get to be part of their lives and support them *as they parent* their kids. By doing this, you have created a community of support that continues to the next generation. They will always be your kids, but as they mature, they can become your friends too.

While pride pushes your kids away, humility gives you the opportunity to win your kids' hearts for life. In the end, humble parenting is not about creating loyal children for ourselves, but rather about releasing our children into the world so they too can make disciples who walk with humility in every area of life. Ultimately, humble parents are willing to send their kids one day into the world on Christ's mission. They join us in the next sphere—the world sphere—as we take the love of Jesus into all the places where we live, work, and play. This is where the humility we've learned in the safety of church and home is put to the test.

Craft Your Family Rule of Life

At the end of Sphere 1, we offered you a step-by-step guide for crafting your personal rule of life. Now we want to help you create your family rule of life. A rule of life, as a reminder, is a one-page bullet-point list that identifies how you believe God wants you to live your life in Christ within your personality. A family rule of life uses the same process to help you identify what life in Christ looks like for your family as a whole given your unique family dynamics and sense of calling.

This worksheet will help clarify your vision as a family. It's a great exercise for couples at any stage of life, with or without kids, and it gives you an opportunity to *work with your spouse* on intentionally creating family culture.

What sort of family do you want to be? What practices and habits do you want to cultivate in your family? Learn more and download this simple step-by-step guide for crafting your family rule of life at TheRevolutionaryDisciple.com/tools. Find the "Crafting Your Family Rule of Life" worksheet and use this exercise to give your family the gift of putting on paper how you envision following Christ together as a family.

THE WORLD SPHERE

*Serve wholeheartedly, as if you were
serving the Lord, not men.*

— Ephesians 6:7

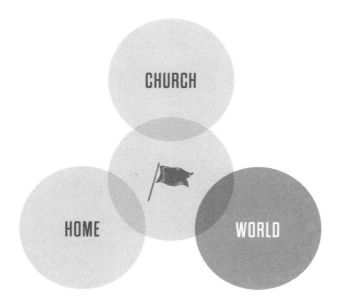

15

POLITICS AND RELIGION

I n the spring of AD 30, Jesus stood in Pilate's courtyard and faced public humiliation. The people of God cast their vote: "Crucify him! Crucify him!" Jesus stood next to a man named Barabbas, as we mentioned, who was a violent rebel. They awaited Pilate's answer. *Which prisoner would Pilate release?* He looked to the people, and the people chose Barabbas over Jesus. This wasn't the first time God's people rejected their true King for someone else.

The prophet Samuel had stood before God's people a millennium earlier, listening to them voice a similar plea. They wanted someone else as king too: "You are old, and your sons do not walk in your ways; now appoint a king to lead us, such as all the other nations have" (1 Sam. 8:5). Samuel was not happy, so he took this request to God.

God replied, "It is not you they have rejected, but they have rejected me as their king" (v. 7). Samuel pleaded with the people, warning them of what their human king would do: exploit them instead of serving them. But the people ignored Samuel. They said, "We want a king over us. Then we will be like all the other nations" (vv. 19–20).

Their kings ruled just as God foretold. Then after God's people lived under a myriad of human kings, God sent his Son to reclaim the throne. Yet the people *rejected God again* when they crucified Jesus. In Samuel's day and in Jesus' day, politics and religion didn't always play well together for the people of God.

Is it any different today? God's people in the church eagerly ask, "Who will be our leader? Who will be our king?" But they're not thinking much about God as their king. *So what does God think about the church's posture toward politics today?*

Politics and Church Collide

As we observe political shifts in North America, some Christians are beginning to feel nauseous, like they're walking the deck of a boat on the open seas. I (Jim) remember going deep sea fishing years ago, when pretty quickly we all knew who was used to the waves—*and who was not.* Me? I hung my head over the side, vomiting along with everyone else who wasn't used to it. The boat workers, however, were used to the open waters, so they had no problem walking, even as the boat constantly shifted. It was life as usual for them.

Political shifts like what we've experienced in recent years will likely become life as usual, but it might take a while to get used to the new normal. While our brothers and sisters in Christ around the world—in places such as China, North Korea, and the Middle East—have learned to deal with hostile political environments, disciples of Jesus in the West have not gotten used to the political and cultural shifts now underway. We'll need to ready our sea legs because this might be a long journey on the open waters.

I (Jim) believe that before Jesus' Second Coming there will be a great falling away—an apostasy (2 Thess. 2:3–9). Jesus says, "The love of most will grow cold" and believers "will be hated by all nations" (Matt. 24:9, 24). Some nations have hated Christians in the past—but Jesus says all nations will hate them. Persecution is in the cards for those who are sincere Christ followers.

As a pastor for more than thirty years, I can tell you it has been especially hard for leaders these days to keep the church unified. It's always been this way, to one degree or another—even in the New

Testament era—but we've seen seismic changes in recent times. In the not-so-distant past, Christians fought over music style, carpet color, and the type of communion trays in church. We've also fought about more serious issues, such as the true origin of the universe, the role of spiritual gifts, and beliefs about end times. But now, new issues are emerging that threaten to devastate our churches. They largely have to do with politics.

As we introduced in Chapter 1, the COVID-19 pandemic was a crucial moment for the world and for our country. The issues became masks or no masks, vaccine or no vaccine, going to church in person or staying home for online services. Every church and family, it seemed, was divided about what to do on all these issues. What were we to do as disciples of Jesus? And those were not the only issues. The US faced riots, looting, protests, police controversies, Critical Race Theory, and the contentious 2020 presidential election.

We were both shocked to see the vitriol among Christians in our country during this time. Churches divided, families split down the middle, and even friendships ended during the chaos. If it wasn't about lockdown protocol, it was over social distancing; if it wasn't over masks, it was over the vaccine; and if it wasn't about reopening businesses, it was about racism. Americans faced a watershed moment in our cultural history, and not everyone fared well. In 2020 divorce rates increased, and church membership fell below 50 percent for the first time on record.[1]

Part of the challenge then, as now, is that we get information from sources that contradict one another. We know fake news exists, but few people agree what qualifies as fake news. Whom can we trust? The coronavirus pandemic amplified that question. Suddenly everyone had a "narrative." People weaponized the media against those with whom they disagreed. They pointed out—and often rightly—cases where the media misled the masses. That's not to mention accusations of collusion, increased censorship on social media, and the rise of cancel culture.

The year 2020 was unlike any other in recent memory. We passed a cultural tipping point, and it seems like there's no going back. It became clear to us, more than at any other period in our lifetimes, how divided our country is—and how divided the church is. Why? Because we began facing conflict between kingdom and country, between politics and religion. We had to answer the question as disciples of Jesus: *Where does our ultimate loyalty lie?*

The Constitution vs. the Scriptures

Take, for example, a meeting I (Jim) had in early 2021 with a military veteran who was a Christian. He had been on three tours to the Middle East and was very upset about the direction our country was headed. He shared with me that he had placed his hand over his heart many times, vowing to defend the Constitution with his life. It had already cost him dearly (suffering from injuries and PTSD), and several of his friends had died on the battlefield. As we talked, he kept quoting the Constitution to justify his anger over governmental changes. He quoted the amendments that supported his rights— rights for which he had fought hard.

I listened and empathized with him that regrettably many people leading in various branches of our government do not view the Constitution the same way. I reminded him that progressives do not see the Constitution as something to be held onto as much as a good place to start from. But I reminded him the Scriptures supersede the Constitution and that our highest Source of truth and authority sits on the throne. My veteran friend had placed the Constitution above the Scriptures in his thinking.

I saw in him what I've begun to see in countless Christians, and it concerns me. When we place our earthly country above our heavenly kingdom, we get all bent out of sorts and confused. When our highest hope lies with our earthly government, then what the government does ultimately becomes unsettling in every part of our lives. In the recent past, people could hide their political views more, but now we cannot hide our politics or religion because they're colliding.

How should we live as disciples of Jesus when our government sometimes leads our country away from what many disciples, including myself, hold dear? This question is not going away anytime soon. To follow Jesus faithfully through the storms, we need a biblical paradigm that's grounded in Scripture. We need Jesus to show us the way of humility.

Jesus in the Face of Governmental Leaders

Jesus challenged the Jewish leaders of his day, who sometimes also carried a political role. Then he allowed the authorities to arrest him and hand him over to the governor of Judea. During his trial, he found himself in the presence of the most powerful ruler in the region, Pontius Pilate, who touted his power to him, "Don't you realize I have power either to free you or to crucify you?" (John 19:10). Notice Jesus' response: "You would have no power over me if it were not given to you from above" (v. 11). Jesus knew even Pilate's authority came from God, so he submitted to the point of death on a cross.

His actions were truly radical for a messiah of that day. But do his actions hold any bearing on us as his disciples? He said to Pilate, "My kingdom is not of this world. If it were, my servants would fight to prevent my arrest by the Jews. *But now my kingdom is from another place*" (John 18:36). He wasn't saying, *We're not going to fight*, but rather, *We're not going to fight that fight. We have a different fight. I'm going to fight the devil, and I'm going to offer my life as a sacrifice.*

Our Lord had a certain way of submitting to the governmental powers while keeping his kingdom first. Even with taxes, Jesus said we're to submit to governmental authorities: "Give to Caesar what is Caesar's, and to God what is God's" (Matt. 22:21). Jesus, the revolutionary, clearly submitted to governmental powers, so what does this mean for us as disciples? Somehow Jesus submitted himself yet never disobeyed God. We have a clear picture of how he acted in front of the "powers that be." But surely we're not expected to submit too, are we? Jesus' actions were unique to his calling as Messiah, right? We don't have to suffer like he did because he already paid the

> *Jesus submitted himself yet never disobeyed God.*

penalty—isn't that the gospel? Before we jump to these conclusions, let's look at how Jesus' earliest disciples interpreted his example in the face of earthly authorities.

The Early Church

The pillar apostle Peter—one of Jesus' closest friends and disciples—took his cues from Jesus, still recognizing injustice when he saw it.

> It is commendable if a man bears up under the pain of unjust suffering because he is conscious of God. But how is it to your credit if you receive a beating for doing wrong and endure it? But if you suffer for doing good and you endure it, this is commendable before God. (1 Peter 2:19–20)

What he says next makes it clear that we're called to emulate Jesus' submission to the powers that be, even when it means unjust suffering in the face of harsh rulers: "To this you were called, because Christ suffered for you, leaving you an example, that you should follow in his steps" (1 Pet. 2:21).[2] Many will point to the Old Testament law, which says, "Eye for eye" when someone mistreats us, but we forget that Jesus also said, "Do not resist *an evil person*" (Matt. 5:38–39). Instead, we're called to turn the other cheek and walk the extra mile (Matt. 5:39–40). The context for these words from Jesus is governmental oppression, where soldiers would mistreat people and force citizens to carry their equipment. Jesus models for us humble submission in the face of unjust suffering.

Paul also showed humility to governmental authority by greeting Roman imperial leaders with their respectful titles (Acts 24:3). When writing to Titus about respecting earthly rulers, he says, "Show *true humility* toward all men" (Titus 3:2), so we see his posture with these and other passages like these. But more importantly, other writings of Paul reveal the same principle of submission to governmental leaders. He delivers pointed instructions for the church.

- "Everyone must submit himself to the governing authorities, for there is no authority except that which God has established" (Rom. 13:1).
- "Remind the people to be subject to rulers and authorities, to be obedient, to be ready to do whatever is good, to slander no one, to be peaceable and considerate, and to show true humility toward all men" (Titus 3:1–2).
- "Submit yourselves for the Lord's sake to every authority instituted among men: whether to the king, as the supreme authority, or to governors, who are sent by him to punish those who do wrong and to commend those who do right" (1 Pet. 2:13–14).

These passages offer clear instructions for the church. But we're still left to work them out in our time and place. We know we're called to submit to governments, yet we also know the highest government ultimately rests on Jesus' shoulders (Isa. 9:6). Jesus is the King of kings and Lord of lords, yet we live under earthly kings and lords. To make matters more complicated, the kingdom of God often functions contrary to the kingdoms of this world. So how do we live in this tension between kingdoms?

> *How do we live in this tension between kingdoms?*

I (Chad) learned a helpful term that describes this tension while living overseas in the Turkish Republic of Northern Cyprus for a brief season in my early twenties. A friend of mine, a native to the island, taught me their Turkish word for political upheaval: *asalabashasha.*

It's a unique word to the Turkish people living on the northern side of Cyprus, and it means "everything turned upside down." It originated in the 1970s when the Cypriots faced immense political upheaval and everything was turned on its head. The Greeks and the Turks had been living together peacefully for generations. Across their small, 140-mile-wide island—throughout the north side and the south side—everyone had a combination of Greek and Turkish neighbors. If you've seen the movie *My Big Fat Greek Wedding*, you know how wild it was for Greeks and Turks to live together as neighbors at all, let alone for decades on end. Everything seemed to be fine, though.

In 1974, however, the island split in two during a cataclysmic civil war. Neighbor turned against neighbor, and everyone had to pick a side—quite literally. As a result, the Greeks gathered to the south and the Turks gathered on the north side of the island.

Asalabashasha. The Turkish Cypriots had their whole world turned upside down all of a sudden, and to this day Cyprus has the only politically divided capital city on the globe. Their civil war changed the very fabric of their society, and the resulting tension remains even now. Although this conflict seemingly arose overnight, it had been brewing for years as separate cultures clashed in shared territory.

This represents the tension many Americans are starting to feel. Something seemed to happen overnight, but it *didn't* happen overnight. The culture wars we're facing now have been brewing for decades, perhaps longer. It feels like now everyone must pick sides on every issue, and suddenly we're a divided country. Even the church feels more divided in some cases. The truth is we've been divided for a long time, and it's just now coming to a head. Can we find a peaceful resolution? Or is it time to fight?

Jim and I strongly believe that if the church will read Acts 4 with Romans 13 together, we can find a wise path forward. If we can learn to hold these passages in balance, they offer us the nuances we need to walk humbly, even though fumbling at times, on the deck of the ship. We are traveling through uncharted waters on the stormy seas, and Scripture, not the Constitution, must be our supreme authority. If the church ever mistook itself for a cruise liner, there's no mistaking it now: we're on a battleship, and it's war. What must we do? Throughout history, Christians have had to deal with this question. Let's walk through the story of Acts 4 and Paul's words in Romans 13 so we can wrestle through this question together.

> *Scripture, not the Constitution, must be our supreme authority.*

16

THE ACTS 4 AND ROMANS 13 PARADIGM

In Acts 4, the Sanhedrin—the Jewish ruling council of the day—commanded Peter and John not to speak about Jesus, because they had been preaching the gospel in the Jewish temple. The Sanhedrin was not a part of the Roman government, but their instructions functioned as law among the people.

How did Peter and John respond? They said, "Judge for yourselves whether it is right in God's sight to obey you rather than God. For we cannot help speaking about what we have seen and heard" (Acts 4:19–20). They refused to stop preaching, no matter what human authority had commanded. They stood up and fought a spiritual battle. Then, on the other hand, we read from Paul in Romans 13:1, "Everyone must submit himself to the governing authorities." We're called to follow God *and* submit ourselves to the governing authorities. How do we resolve this tension?

We know that Jesus faced this internal battle and chose to deny himself and his rights—and to obey his Father's will to the end. He was wronged, yet he did not defend himself. He died physically because he knew the everlasting spiritual realm and the eventual new heaven and new earth were at stake for the human race. Yet he fought the right kinds of battles and taught his disciples to do the same. So how do we live with humility in light of these examples?

We propose what we call the Acts 4 and Romans 13 paradigm. We believe that if disciples of Jesus will wholeheartedly seek to understand and apply these two passages, they will walk away with an approach that's anchored in Scripture, balanced, and clear. In the end, we hope this paradigm will help us all successfully navigate a myriad of difficult issues in the world sphere.

Acts 4: Standing Up

In Acts 4, Peter and John's actions show disciples how to stand up for God before the authorities. Let's keep in mind that by this time Peter, for example, had worked through some of his personal pride and fear. So he was ready to follow Jesus' example all the way to his own death. His form of fighting was no longer to pick up a sword. He had already tried that and was rebuked by Jesus (John 18:11). He eventually would die for his faith, and in so doing, helped change the history of the world without a physical army. Why? Because the authorities contradicted what Jesus *had expressly commanded them to do in the Great Commission*—to go and make disciples.

Now, I (Jim) believe there is such thing as a just war, even if it's not what we should do first, second, or even third. Physical war is justified if the purpose is to protect the innocent.[3] I have honored and prayed for many soldiers and police officers who legally and humbly gave of themselves for others. What a worthy profession to have! There is a time when citizens fight physically as an act of courage against ungodly oppression. However, Christians don't go around looking for a fight because we're called to be peacemakers and people who seek peace (Matt. 5:9; 1 Pet. 3:11). We are filled with the Holy Spirit, and the fruit of his presence is peace (Gal. 5:22–23).

So what do we do with Acts 4? When do we say no to people and yes to God? Humble disciples of Jesus say no *only when people are asking us to do something that is clearly contrary to God's expressed commands in Scripture.* For Peter and John, they had been commanded to preach the gospel, so preach they did.

Now, non-believers may villainize Christians no matter what we do, as they have for millennia. But we seek to bring glory to Jesus by honoring him, his Word, and by being led by his Spirit to love others—even our enemies. Here's the key: we should never fight like the devil for the things of God.

> *We should never fight like the devil for the things of God.*

I (Chad) believe one way we can take our stand is by using our right to free speech through the legal system when necessary. If a Christian faces legal prosecution, for example, they should make their case respectfully and intelligibly. That's how Peter and John did it. They went to prison, appeared in court, and answered their accusers with respectful but direct words. They started with, "Rulers and elders of the people!" and then made their case (Acts 4:8). The Jewish council didn't like what Peter and John were doing, but Peter and John's humble and incisive rhetoric dumbfounded the rulers. The rulers released them, for the time being, and the apostles kept preaching. We can study this example and take notes. In the end, though, we must be prepared to suffer for the gospel like they did (see Acts 5:12–40). Like them, we don't put our hope in whether or not the courts agree with us or pass good and right laws. We live faithfully to God no matter what.

We reject the sort of attitude I (Jim) once saw portrayed on a car bumper. On one side of the bumper, the sticker said, "My boss is a Jewish carpenter," and on the other side it said, "If you want my gun, you'll have to pry it out of my cold, lifeless fingers." Somehow the owner of this car had come to believe that a Christian could be characterized by rebellion in the world and still be called a disciple who says to Jesus, "Lord, Lord." Don't get me wrong. I have a lot of guns because I'm a hunter, but Scripture makes it clear that if the government asks me to do something and it doesn't clearly contradict God's Word, I'm to submit and obey those authorities.

As you can see, this paradigm has nuances, and we must learn to live in those nuances. Take Paul's life, for example. He used his rights as a Roman citizen to testify before the courts throughout the land, including eventually Emperor Nero. He always spoke respectfully and made a clear and logical argument (Acts 22:1–21; 25:8–11; 26:2–27). Yet he refused to worship Nero as a god—and was beheaded for it. For him, a time came to say no to human authority. But when we read his testimonies in Acts, we see how he "fought"—*with humility*. These nuances can be challenging to navigate. Thankfully, we have, in addition to his life's story, Paul's thoughts on this topic in his letter to the Romans.

Romans 13: Sitting Down

In Romans 13, Paul emphasizes humility before governmental leaders. So how do we balance the resistance we see in Acts 4 with the instructions to submit in Romans 13? In this passage, the apostle Paul tells us *that we should submit to earthly leaders* because they have been placed there by God.

> Everyone must submit himself to the governing authorities, for there is no authority except that which God has established. The authorities that exist have been established by God. Consequently, he who rebels against the authority is rebelling against what God has instituted, and those who do so will bring judgment on themselves. (Romans 13:1–2)

In the context, Paul spoke to Christians living in Rome under pagan leaders. For Paul, to rebel against them *was to rebel against God.*[4]

At this point in the discussion, Christians like to talk about the Second Amendment, which reads, "A well regulated Militia, being necessary to the security of a free State, the right of the people to keep and bear Arms, shall not be infringed." How we interpret this is not the main issue. The main issue is that many Christians are more familiar with this amendment than they are with Romans 13.

Before we quote the Constitution or the Bill of Rights, disciples ought to go to the authority of God's Word first to express our highest loyalty to him. Romans 13 is clear: *"Everyone must submit himself to the governing authorities, for there is no authority except that which God has established"* (Rom. 13:1). Jesus modeled for us what submission looks like during his trial before the Jewish and

Roman governmental leaders. So if Christ walked with humility in the midst of false accusations, physical persecution, and even unjust prosecution, then we too are to walk humbly with him, even in this area of life.

You might at this point say, "If we give them our guns now, they will come for our Bibles next." This could be true, but no matter what happens, we will be able to handle anything through Christ who gives us strength (Phil. 4:13). This world was never our home, and Paul was right to say it "is better by far" to go and be with the Lord than to stay on this planet, even in the best of circumstances (Phil. 1:23).

We humbly follow Jesus even if this doesn't make sense to us. We don't have to understand or agree with Jesus to follow him. This is a case in point about humility. When, not if, we disagree with leaders, what we do is important. And how we talk to them and about them is important too. This applies to governmental leaders, a boss at work, church leaders, and others. Just because we disagree with them doesn't mean we get a free ticket to slander or gossip about them. In Ephesians, Paul says, "Do not let any unwholesome talk come out of your mouths" (Eph. 4:29). What good does it do anyway to post angry messages on social media and rant to our friends?

What if we spent that energy on praying for those who have angered us instead? Scripture clearly tells us to pray for governmental leaders: "I urge . . . that requests, prayers, intercession and thanksgiving be made for everyone—for kings and all those in authority, that we may live peaceful and quiet lives in all godliness and holiness" (1 Tim. 2:1–2). When we pray for the government, we pray most of all for peace. Why? Immediately after this call to pray, Paul says of our peaceful lives, "This is good, and pleases God our Savior, who wants all men to be saved" (vv. 3–4). The gospel is at stake in the world, and our prayers can make a difference. When you're tempted to rebel or slander, remember that Jesus came to save *all people* and, according to Scripture, peace is God's pathway to salvation, not war.

> Peace is God's pathway to salvation, not war.

Is There a Limit to Humble Submission?

I (Jim) have deeply considered the implications of what we're saying here. You may or may not agree with me about our position. You may say I am too much of a pacifist for your liking. Or you may say I am inconsistent by saying there is a place to fight physically. For my more nationalistic friends, let us be clear again that there are limits to our submission. If anyone asks us to sin against God or do something clearly contrary to the teachings of God in Scripture, we must not submit. But we also cannot merely act as though these passages about submission don't exist.

We embrace the Acts 4 and Romans 13 paradigm, which holds both sides of this issue in tension. We have to wrestle with these passages and make *God's Word the center of our worldview*. So limits exist, but we must let *Scripture identify what those limitations are*— just like in every other area of life. For example, Paul tells women to submit to their husbands "in everything" (Eph. 5:24). But wives shouldn't submit to their husbands without boundaries or qualifications. They still obey God above their husbands. It's the same with government.

Let us also be clear that while these passages about government make it plain that God has sovereignly distributed, or has at least allowed, humans to have authority, this doesn't mean God chooses specific governmental leaders. It simply means that their position is worthy of our respect and submission. Neither does this mean we must submit to their particular ideology or agree with their policies. This is the balance: as long as governmental laws *do not conflict* with God's *clear commands* in Scripture, we submit ourselves to them.

This means that when the government makes a law, we don't break it. We don't:

- Break the speed limit
- Take illegal drugs
- Pirate media
- Cheat on taxes
- Neglect construction regulations

- Go hunting without a license
- Drink alcohol underage

You get the idea. We abide by the laws of the land. Our goal by listing these here is not to list all the laws or tease out all the nuances of the above passages but to show you the general principle in Scripture of submitting to governmental authority.

The bottom line is that when it comes to government, we must all ask ourselves: *Does God's Word tell us that God has established governmental authority?* The answer is clearly yes, but Romans 13 *does not mean* that God ordains everything governmental authorities do. We all know that governments go to war against one another, and God is not divided. So he cannot ordain all governmental action. God ordained governance, not governments.[5] Christians generally want an all-or-nothing approach to this God and government dynamic, but it's not that simple. We want either an "I reject the government" approach or an "I'm always for government" approach. But God's Word doesn't support either of those.

> God ordained governance, not governments.

God's Word shows us that the general spirit of a believer is to live humbly in an attitude of submission to governmental authorities as well as to bosses, spouses, and so on, rather than in prideful rebellion. In practical terms, this means we follow laws, give honor to governmental authorities, and show respect to political leaders. Disciples of Jesus generally obey all authority—the only exception, again, being when a leader asks us to do something *clearly contradictory* to God's Word. Then we choose to obey God's Word instead of people. The progression goes like this:

1. Decide the kingdom of your primary loyalty (your earthly nation or the kingdom of God).
2. Immerse yourself in God's Word about humble submission to the government.

3. When rebellion arises in your heart, recognize it, and take captive every thought, making it obedient to Christ. Rather than giving in to emotion, allow God's Spirit to work through your mind to seek God's view and his direction.
4. Determine if you're being asked to do something *clearly contradictory to the Word*.
5. Humbly live out your convictions in the world when you're compelled by God's Word, but only if the two clearly and explicitly contradict one another. Otherwise, submit to leaders.
6. Live peaceably with people in the church with whom you disagree about any disputable matter.

That last piece about living peaceably while disagreeing with others in the church can be the most challenging part. But this too is vital. If we're to be united as a church, what do we do amidst sharp disagreements?

The Acts 4 and Romans 13 paradigm works well—until we disagree. Mask or no mask? Vaccine or no vaccine? Mature Christians disagree about questions like these, so how do we live together in unity? While reading Acts 4 and Romans 13 together helps us decide how to walk humbly in the world, we have the added challenge of figuring out how to walk humbly in the church *with those who decide differently than us.* Unity is easy when we agree, but what about when we disagree?

Romans 14: Disputable Matters

In Romans 14, Paul provides another way to help us think through what he calls "disputable matters" (v. 1). Some issues are not disputable, like whether or not to preach the gospel, or whether or not it's okay to get drunk (Eph. 5:18). But what about having one drink of alcohol? Christians have different opinions, perspectives, and convictions on this issue and many more. In Paul's day, the church in Rome wrestled through what foods were okay to eat due to various pagan and Jewish customs. In our day, we wrestle with our own issues. It's interesting how disputable matters often have to do with our bodies.

Good people will always disagree about some issues, and we are allowed to have different opinions! That's what's beautiful about Romans 14. Paul says about disputable issues, "Let us . . . make every effort to do what leads to peace and to mutual edification" (Rom. 14:19). God prioritizes unity in disputable matters. Rupertus Meldenius summarized it this way: "In essentials unity, in non-essentials liberty, in all things charity." While this quote is often attributed to more well-known theologians, Meldenius originally used it. He was a seventeenth-century theologian who included this statement in his tract about Christian unity when European Christians of his day were divided about politics and religion.[6] This shows how our current struggles are nothing new. In our day, as in many times in the past, disciples must ensure that external matters do not divide the church.

I (Jim) often feel the struggle between the world and the church, and I always want to make a place within the family of God where people can experience peace and safety. Many people truly love Jesus but struggle with how to handle abrupt shifts away from Christian values on the political landscape. That's why I hold up Romans 14 as a lightning rod for Christians in confusing times like these. Paul begins, "Accept him whose faith is weak, without passing judgment on disputable matters" (Rom. 14:1). He provides a framework for disagreements within the church; and even in disputable matters, we can unite on the following principles from Romans 14:

1. Discern from Scripture which matters are disputable and which are not (Rom. 14). The importance of the gospel, the necessity of salvation, and the command to follow Jesus are not disputable matters.
2. Do not fight over disputable matters (Rom. 14:1–4). Discussion has its place, but never divisive fighting within the body of Christ.

3. Then—and this is the key—do not judge those in the church with whom you disagree about these disputable matters.

When a matter is disputable, be fully convinced in your conscience what you think is right and follow your conscience to avoid sin (Rom. 14:5, 23). But as you do, be humble with others who disagree with you. If someone else has a different opinion, let that be between them and God. Keep your opinion private when possible, so as not to create division in the church (Rom. 14:22).

We challenge disciples in our churches to look intently into this Scripture and others to discover how we should live in light of them. As we work out the nuances of when to stand and when to sit now and in the coming years, we will continue to feel strongly that disorientation caused by a moving ship. Many are stumbling into one another—even shoving, fighting, or falling flat on their faces. So we urge you now: study the Scriptures on this topic in this chapter and other Scriptures on this topic to let God help you navigate these waters.

> *Remember your rights are not as important as your relationships.*

In this whole discussion, remember your rights are not as important as your relationships. In the end, you might have rights as a citizen of your country, but you have no right to demand that other believers agree with you on disputable matters. God wants unity in his church. The bottom line is this: in essentials unity, in non-essentials liberty, and in all things love.

So when does the disciple of Jesus revolt? We hope you see now how that question misses the point. Rather, the point is this: How can we walk humbly with Jesus in the midst of a broken world? Learning a Christlike posture toward the government lays the groundwork for walking through other areas of the world sphere, such as work and play.

17

THE HUMBLE BOSS AND WORKER

I (Jim) remember what the elders said to me one night when I was at my wits' end. I was serving at a church as a young youth minister, and they expected me to do what I thought was part of *their job*—to pastor the adults. At the time, I was in charge of 150 kids, including junior high and high school students and young adults. And that's not even taking into account the time and energy needed to deal with their parents. Then the elders asked me to pastor even more people. That's when the workload and unrealistic expectations began to impact my family negatively. *What does humble submission look like then?* I wondered.

Everything came to a head one night during a meeting when the elders said, "You know what? We need to start a home group system. Jim, you're going to be the head of that system."

I already made very little money, worked two jobs, and was overloaded. My wife worked two jobs too, and I didn't have any more time to give to the church without it severely taking a toll on my family. As they brought up yet another area for me to oversee, I remember thinking, *What does God call us to do when our boss asks us to do what's unreasonable?*

I said, "Okay, I'll do it, but to truly pastor and shepherd them, if there are problems, I will also send people to you guys to shepherd and pastor as the elders of the church."

An elder said, "No, you won't. That's what we're paying *you to do*," implying my job would be on the line for giving out their phone numbers.

What was I supposed to do now? They were being unreasonable! I was about to blow a gasket. My dad had already discipled me on how to submit to bad leaders, so I followed what he taught me in this new situation.

"Okay," I said. "I'll do my best. I don't know how I can do that and have a healthy family, but I'll find a way." I knew I had to create boundaries because I was determined not to sacrifice my family on the altar of ministry.

Sitting with the elders that night, I tried hard not to react negatively, knowing how I had done that in the past. This time, I put my head down and submitted to their unreasonable request as best as I could by rethinking my schedule: *Am I in the wrong? Is there a better way to do the job that I don't know about? Do I need wise counsel?* These were the types of questions a humble person asks, even though I didn't feel humble in the moment. I'll be honest—the posture of Christlike humility wasn't at all natural for me (and still isn't in my sinful nature). But I knew I had to take the humble path, so I asked my dad to help me through it.

My dad suggested that maybe the reason I couldn't do more was because of the way I was leading. So for about a year, I tried different ways of leading. I modified my style, raised up volunteers, and the church even agreed to hire another youth minister to help me out. The church continued to grow, but I eventually maxed out again. We faced a crossroads: the elders refused to serve and I refused to let ministry at church become more important than my ministry at home. So we eventually had to split ways. But my dad's counsel kept me level-headed through it all; he urged me to take the humble path and not react in anger. I'm so grateful to this day for his wisdom as I learned what it looks like to walk humbly in the work sphere.

During my early ministry years in situations like these, I had to sort this out: what's my response when an elder or senior pastor asks me to do something unreasonable in my mind? This kind of thing is somewhat expected in the world, but it's especially surprising when it happens in the church.

During my first ten years in ministry, I worked under senior pastors and elders as "my bosses." Plus, I had many secular jobs before I became senior pastor at Real Life Ministries in Idaho. So I learned the challenges of working under someone else in both ministry and non-ministry contexts. Work experiences at churches can actually be more challenging than out in the real world because church leaders ought to know better—and act better. The devil has a good time making a mess at our secular jobs, *but he has a heyday* meddling with the church. He uses our pride to tempt us toward rebellion. We must actively fight for humility in the work world.

Overcoming Pride as an Employee

We often talk about "taking pride in our work," but that's different than *having pride at work*. Pride at work causes major damage in our lives. So why do we let our pride do this? It happens to us both as employees and as leaders. Those working for someone else can make it all about them—what *they* want, what *they* think is right, how much *they* get paid, and what credit *they* get for their contribution.

Do you find yourself thinking that way sometimes? Pride can flare up when our boss tells us to do something we don't like (or we don't agree with), like in my story with the elders. In that case, I chose the humble path, but it took everything in me, wise counsel, and God's grace to help me through it. I knew by that point in my life that pride just doesn't work. No one likes to work with someone who can't be coached, critiqued, or trained.

The apostle Paul paints the picture of humility in the workplace in Ephesians. His words might be shocking because of our modern lenses about slavery, yet they're still instructive for us.

> Slaves, obey your earthly masters with respect and fear,
> and with sincerity of heart, just as you would obey Christ.
> Obey them not only to win their favor when their eye is on
> you, but like slaves of Christ, doing the will of God from
> your heart. Serve wholeheartedly, as if you were serving the
> Lord, not men, because you know that the Lord will reward
> everyone for whatever good he does, whether he is slave or free.
> (Ephesians 6:5–8)

Paul tells us here we should work with integrity and humility no
matter what—even if we're not appreciated. Why? Because what we
do is for the Lord. We'll be rewarded by the Lord even when others
don't reward us. Those words must have been
so healing and hopeful to slaves who heard

We'll be rewarded by the Lord even when others don't reward us.

them, especially those living in difficult conditions. We hope they bring you comfort and
strength as well. But were slaves really supposed to grin and bear it like this?

When I (Jim) took a philosophy class
at North Idaho College, I was taught that the Bible is "racist" and
"endorses slavery." So let's be clear about this: Paul never endorsed
slavery. *He acknowledged slavery existed* and provided guidance for
how to live within it when they could not change it, but that's different than endorsing it. In fact, Paul encouraged slaves who could
gain freedom to do so (1 Cor. 7:21). He knew what was in his control and what was not. Plus, slavery had little to do with race at that
time, which made it different than US slave history. We do not condone slavery of any kind, nor do we support it as an institution.
We also do not stand for any sort of abuse at work or in any other
context. Yet we can talk about humility at work from this passage
because of overlap between the life of slaves back then and that of
workers today.[7]

Just like then, we might have a non-Christian boss over us. We
know in Paul's day most slaves worked for unbelievers and some were
mistreated by physical abuse or neglected with regard to receiving

basic necessities.[8] Yet Paul still called them to be obedient and walk in humility. Most workers today don't face the same treatment, so how much more should we be able to apply these instructions to our context!

In Ephesians 6, Paul tells his audience to come under their boss in the workplace:

- with respect (v. 5)
- with fear (v. 5)
- with sincerity of heart (v. 5)
- as they would obey Christ (v. 5)
- all the time (v. 6)
- with their whole heart (v. 7)

Notice how these words connect with humility: respect, fear, sincerity of heart, obey, and serve. We're called as workers to be humble and obedient. What's remarkable is that Paul doesn't add any conditions or exceptions. He simply says, "Obey your earthy masters . . . just as you would obey Christ."

From our experience, learning to obey an earthly boss trains us to obey God. So it goes both ways: discipleship to Jesus makes us better workers, and learning submission at work helps us better submit to Jesus. Perhaps that's why God ordained us to spend most of our waking hours at work! He knew it'd give us ample opportunity to learn humility. This sounds pretty easy, but what about when we have a bad boss?

When We're Mistreated at Work

I (Chad) worked at a mobile paper shredding company in Nashville, Tennessee, when I was fresh out of college. Four of us employees shredded the paper, and our boss was the general manager. I remember walking into some of the businesses we serviced to pick up paper for mobile shredding and laughing to myself when the customers would sometimes call over the loudspeaker, upon seeing my garb,

"The shredder is here." I had never imagined being called "the shredder" in my career.

Well, apparently, not everyone could handle the perception of the job because the most senior paper shredder quit in flying colors one day. I pulled into the facility and saw skid marks in the parking lot where this guy had peeled out. My boss told me he had quit— and didn't leave well. Whatever his issue, I know he hadn't been *mistreated on the job*. Perhaps he let his anger get the best of him; maybe it was his pride. Whatever it was, he let everyone know he was better than that job. I'll admit it was a shot to my pride to earn a living by shredding paper with a college degree in hand. I was tempted to think I was too good for the job. But what gave me a leg up was having an example of humility in Jesus Christ. Just knowing that Jesus "did not come to be served, but to serve" gave me a vision for humility at work (Matt. 20:28). Shredding paper was an opportunity to serve.

My former coworker is an example of anger on the job without mistreatment, but how do disciples of Christ not get angry and quit *when they are mistreated?* We must say it again that we condemn abuse and harassment. But how do we humbly respond to unreasonable requests? Submitting to leaders who treat us well is easy, but what about when they treat us poorly? How do we submit in reverence to Christ and not react in anger or fear?

Let us be clear: there is a time to report mistreatment, abuse, or harassment, or to quit a job if you're being asked to sin. Sometimes, you must make those hard decisions. But even so, you have to walk through these situations prayerfully, tempering them with respect and an attitude of humility. Don't peel out on your way out! Quit with humility and not without prayer and wise counsel. You don't get a pass on emotional outbursts. Angry fits of rage only damage your witness to those around you. Rather than showing wrathful anger, deal with your anger in a righteous way. You can set right boundaries, and you should. But do it in the right way.

Perhaps, for whatever reason, you have believed that faith is separate from your work life, and "never the twain shall meet." If that's you, peel back the layers and let God change your heart about your work life because there's no separation like that in Scripture. What does this look like in practical terms?

The Humble Worker

Take some advice for walking humbly with your boss. Ready? We warn you these may not feel natural.

1. Follow your boss even when they're being unreasonable. Even when they are not fair in how they pay or promote people, for example, still follow your boss. Again, there's a right time and place for voicing concern, reporting mistreatment, and advocating for reform. Yet if we're following Christ, we must be humble in it all. We may not understand, but that doesn't keep us from humbly doing our work. Remember that "the Lord will reward everyone for whatever good he does" (Eph. 6:8). So eventually we can look forward to God's reward—which is worth remembering.

2. Follow your boss when nobody's looking. This practice of secret integrity offers an excellent opportunity to learn sincerity of heart. It's also a good way to unlearn people-pleasing and relearn God-pleasing. Ultimately, God is our master. If we're serving him and aiming to please him, we won't do things just to please people but also to please God. So keep your commitments at work, let your boss lead, and follow them. This type of integrity brings great peace and satisfaction. We reveal our true way of life when no one's looking.

3. Follow your boss wholeheartedly. Just like we're to love God with our whole heart, God expects us to follow our earthly bosses wholeheartedly too. This trains us how to serve God better. Work gives us ample opportunity to understand what it means to serve others with all our being. God uses the workplace to form our character and to teach us how to love him and other people better—not just at work but in every sphere.

Humility with Authority

Paul next addresses those who have authority in the workplace.

And masters, treat your slaves in the same way. Do not threaten them, since you know that he who is both their Master and yours is in heaven, and there is no favoritism with him. (Ephesians 6:9)

Bosses are to treat their workers "in the same way," but in the same way as what? In the context of this passage, it's serving their workers wholeheartedly, just as Paul instructed slaves to serve their masters wholeheartedly. This is a total reversal of how worldly cultures think about "being in charge" at work.

This comes back to our definition of a humble disciple: knowing who we are before God and *choosing to go lower*. Even when we gain a position of authority, we're to be proactive in laying down our rights, going lower, and serving. Jesus held the highest position of authority, and even he came to serve. We might be a lead pastor, children's minister, CEO, mid-level manager, or a dispatch officer for a trucking company. No matter our position, there's no escaping the path of humility. Even when we get to the top of our industry, in Christ we're called to walk back down the humble path of discipleship to the bottom.

I (Chad) have a friend who stepped onto a Southwest airplane, took a seat, and found himself sitting next to a prominent Southwest employee—at the very back of the plane.[9] He found out she was not just any employee of Southwest; she was the CFO of the entire airline! She intentionally chose one of the last seats on the plane, even though she had every right to sit wherever she wanted. My friend chatted with her the whole flight, and when they landed, he thanked her for showing servant leadership.

She responded, "You are too kind. As a part of the leadership team at Southwest, it is important to us to understand our customers because we have been in their shoes. I hope that never changes." This CFO served as a great example of knowing one's identity. She was so confident in her identity that she didn't feel as if she had to earn her position, protect it, or announce it. Notice that *she chose to go lower.* I have no knowledge of her relationship with God to tell if she's a disciple, but even if that's how a non-disciple acted, how much more should followers of Jesus live with humility in the world!

Perhaps the call to humility is even greater for those at the top because there's more space between their position and the bottom. That's why the incarnation of Christ is so amazing. Christ came from his high position in heaven to our low place on earth. Jesus showed himself as a servant leader. Yet God exalts the humble, as he did with Christ, who "has gone into heaven and is at God's right hand—with angels, authorities and powers in submission to him" (1 Pet. 3:22). Jesus now reigns with authority and humility! And when we willingly lay down our rights and authority at work, we display the glory of Christ in the world. Sounds easy, right? Unfortunately, pride makes this easy to understand but hard to live out.

> *The call to humility is even greater for those at the top.*

What Proud Leaders Look Like at Work

Perhaps you're a leader at work. Maybe those under you don't work hard enough, or they aren't working the way you want them to. Pride tempts us to look out for ourselves as the top priority, and everyone else becomes our servants or tools to be used. We would never say that, but we might think, *These people exist for me, my goals, and my career.* Jesus warns us about this mentality:

> The rulers of the Gentiles lord it over them, and their high officials exercise authority over them. Not so with you. Instead, whoever wants to become great among you must be your servant, and whoever wants to be first must be your slave. (Matthew 20:25–27)

Jesus makes the point that even bosses *are supposed to become slaves!* Is Jesus really telling us to be slaves here? While slavery was different in his day than in US history, as we've mentioned, slaves still lived an undesirable life of servitude. A slave was and is someone entirely dedicated to serving others. This teaching about "becoming slaves" in the workplace calls for a radical rethinking of our roles in the world. When we take on the humility of Christ as his disciples, we voluntarily became a slave to all. That's a big commitment! So either way—whether we're a worker or a leader of others—we're to be servants at work.

We must be servants, that is, even when we're leaders. Pride looks like a manager who decides to sling to others all the stuff their boss slings at them. They treat employees like indentured servants. As disciples, though, we're called to be the servant. Remember, a humble disciple knows who they are before God—even in a position of power—*and chooses to go lower.*

Maybe you've learned how to serve humbly at church and at home, but what about at work? Even if your job is working for a church, you can put on your Sunday face as a church leader. But what about behind closed doors forty to sixty hours a week? How do you treat employees? Other staff members? What about volunteers? Are they your servants or are you theirs? Satan loves it when Christians think they're mature in all spheres of life but hold on to one area—like work—and silo it from sanctification. What does it look like to love people at your work with humility when you're a leader? Let's keep talking.

The Actions of a Humble Leader

Being a godly boss and serving at work doesn't mean that you necessarily agree with an employee's perspective. And a good boss expects those who work for them to do a good job. They arrange employees in ways that serve the mission of a business. As a leader, you often have a larger perspective than those who work for you—or at least you should if you're in charge! You know how solutions are not as simple as others in the company or organization might think. And you may have people you answer to as well, so you're not just a boss but also an employee.

As a manager, then, you're obligated to respond to the thoughts and feelings of your boss while also considering those under you. With all this in mind, consider these insights to help you walk in humility at work.

1. You're in a position of responsibility rather than privilege. Use your position for the overall good of the people you serve (your customer or client), as well as those on your team. And seek to see things from others' perspectives, not just your own. Even if you don't agree with them, listen to them. Hearing and agreeing are not the same thing.

2. Use your job as your mission field. Remember God's goal for your role is not just for you to make a living but also to work in such a way that draws people to him. As a disciple of Jesus, you are the light of the world. Your goal is not just business success but also kingdom success. You are following Jesus, being changed by Jesus, and a fisher of people. Bloom where you're planted in the mission field of work.

> *Bloom where you're planted in the mission field of work.*

3. Are you growing in humility? As a leader, what you do speaks more than how you create a team culture. You're not going to be humble in every circumstance with a flawless record, but is humility even on your radar at work? Do you know when you're being proud and justifying it? Identify where you are and take the next step to grow.

I (Jim) want to say that our goal with work is not praise from people but from God. This is especially important for those who work in ministry. At times, a leader's work feels mundane and thankless. People don't recognize our good work; instead, they often pick at us. When that happens, look to Christ, who didn't run away when work got hard but instead laid "down his life for the sheep" (John 10:11). Like Christ, our goal is to lay down our lives for those we serve. Rest in seeking God's approving words, "Well done, good and faithful servant" (Matt. 25:21). When you keep your eyes on that end goal, you can live your life without depending on accolades from people. This focus helps at work, but the world sphere is not just about who we are before the government and at work. It's also about who we are as we play.

18

HUMILITY AT PLAY

On June 29, 1983, Kansas City Chiefs running back Joe Delaney attempted to rescue three children who were drowning in a pond in Monroe, Louisiana. When Joe saw the children drowning in the pond, he dove in to save them. But Joe couldn't swim. He tried to save the children, but only one of the three children survived the incident. Joe Delaney drowned in the process of trying to save the others.[10]

You've likely never heard of Joe Delaney because he only played two years in the NFL, but ESPN featured him in their special *30 for 30* documentary series—because of his talent, yes, but more because of who he was as a person. He had been the fastest NFL player his rookie season in 1981 and won Rookie of the Year. During his first two years with the Chiefs, he set two franchise records that stood for more than twenty years. He had a promising career with the Kansas City Chiefs on the horizon.

But his character is what made him special. As his heroism showed, he didn't consider sports to be the most important part of life. His former teammate, Deron Cherry, said of him, "He was proud of what he accomplished, but yet it didn't go to his head. He was the same Joe Delaney before he was a Rookie of the Year . . . and even afterwards, he was still the same guy." Joe's wife said that he "never cashed a check, whether it was in the NFL or a regular job. He would always bring the check and give it to me. He said, 'Hey, this is yours. Just give me a little change to put in my pocket so if I want to stop by the store, I can get a Coke. I'm happy with that.'"[11] He was more concerned about others than himself.

That's why he tried to save the children at the park. While he was a pro athlete, his life was characterized by serving and putting others first. He valued sports, play, and fun, but he didn't live for those. A reporter once asked him about his ability, "Are you fast?" He replied, "Yeah, I am." But he was not arrogant. His talent was obvious to everyone, and he simply acknowledged that. While we don't know whether or not he was a disciple of Jesus, we know that his life showed the characteristics of a humble disciple: he knew who he was and lowered himself for the sake of serving others—even to the point of death. While he set records and won awards, the world now remembers Joe Delaney because of his character.

Humble People Play

We play through sports, music, art, and the like, but what does play have to do with discipleship? Must we really learn to submit to God at play? Does God even care what we do in sports, for example, other than have fun? It might seem odd, but this area also lies within the journey of discipleship.

As the Gospel of Matthew recounts, Jesus laid his hands on the kids who were brought to him. But this was not without struggle! His disciples tried to interfere. They rebuked those bringing the kids to Jesus for a blessing. Jesus said, "Let the little children come to me, and do not hinder them, for the kingdom of heaven belongs to such as these" (Matt. 19:14). At the most basic level, this story shows us the capacity children have for knowing God. Like Jesus' disciples, we as parents sometimes move our kids out of the way for the more "serious business" of discipleship. Yet discipleship includes play, and perhaps that's part of what Jesus is getting at here. The children were not the problem; instead, the adults were. For Jesus, discipleship was for children too.

I (Chad) have heard it said that you can learn more about a person by watching them play for an hour than by talking with them for a year. I think that's true! I appreciate how G. K. Chesterton describes how prideful people can settle into a "sort of selfish seriousness" in life.[12] So the first step for us is to have a place to play. Then we must allow God to make us humble even when our guard's down because we're having fun. If we let our guard down anywhere, it's at play, so pride is sure to show up in all sorts of ways. This includes everything from our kids' activities to our own hobbies.

Though some people don't make time for hobbies, most of us have one. For those with kids or grandkids, however, this discussion is more about how we act around our children and others at sporting events, music venues, or extracurricular activities. These activities offer a great playing field for becoming spiritually mature because we can give God even our playful self, our surface-level self, and perhaps even our competitive self. Why is it so important to learn humility when we play? Our holiness, testimony, and even our child's character development are at stake.

> *We can give God even our playful self.*

I (Chad) appreciate Gerard Manley Hopkins's poem "As Kingfishers Catch Fire," which inspired Eugene Peterson's book title by that name. Hopkins reminds us not to separate our faith from the rest of life "for Christ plays in ten thousand places."[13] Not only do we play outside of the four walls of the church, but we know *Christ also plays with us and he can work in us when we play.* Christ can transform us into his image in the Sunday service and in the soccer game. This isn't always easy.

The Most Important Part of Play

I (Jim) understand the challenge of discipling kids who play sports since I have three boys who were active in sports. For me, the greatest challenge was teaching my boys how to be humble and respectful when I thought their coach wasn't doing a good job coaching. The fact that I didn't think coaches did it right gives you a hint as to why this area is challenging for me—my pride.

Although I coached many teams after my competitive wrestling days were over, I didn't always coach my sons' teams. At times, it took everything inside of me to keep my cool when one of their coaches didn't understand the game very well. The worst was when a coach would put their own kid into the game at a crucial time, even when it wasn't in the team's best interest. While the temptation might be to make a change or to step in and take control, these pure-hearted intentions can often turn into ugly conflicts in sports.

Parents too often treat the Little Leagues like the Major Leagues. It's pretty obvious their top priority is winning. Of course, winning is fun and even a great goal, but when this gets in the way of more important priorities, it starts to turn ugly. Keeping priorities straight is especially challenging because parents and kids both want to win! Yet the most important aspect of play is not winning but character development, and if we don't respect a coach or a teacher in front of the kids (even when we disagree with them), we're not teaching our kids humility. Every kid needs to learn how to respect authority and submit, even when they don't agree with the person in authority. At play, we learn what to do when we don't get the outcome we want. When we learn to accept a shared goal instead of a personal one, we can willingly give up our personal desires for the good of the team.

Prideful outbursts happen, even among Christians, when a parent tries to "fix" a bad situation, for example. They think, *Okay, I'm going to fix this so my kid can have more fun.* As a result, they unintentionally start a small rebellion, or perhaps cause a team to split and form a new team. Conflict and in-fighting display pride in a parent. Behavior like this speaks volumes to kids, showing them that winning is the number-one priority. Sure, your kid may get more playing time if you put up a fight—and they may even win more games—but what happens to their soul? You form a Little League coup for Christ, and suddenly, it goes south. This happens all the time, and it can ruin your kid's character development in sports and your Christian testimony in the world.

A Coup for Christ

I (Jim) remember the conversation with a set of football-loving parents who came to our church. The dad told us the coach of their kids' team didn't know what he was doing. But instead of working it out and sticking with the team, the dad went to the league organizer and said, "I'm going to pull my kid from the team, and all the parents are on my side—unless you replace the coach *with me*."

He was known as a Christian in the community, which really caused a stink among other parents. But he still followed through with it! This little rebellion gave Christians a bad name in the league.

Is that what Christ has called us to? To let him reign in every area of our lives *except when we play*? No! In Christ, we're called to give him everything and to be humble like him. In sports, for example, this looks like teaching our kids to:

- Play by the rules of the game.
- Show up on time.
- Help others who've fallen down.
- Be respectful to referees and other players.
- Listen to instruction from their coaches.
- Admit their mistakes.
- Display good sportsmanship.

All of these actions and more come back to the core practices of humility: serving, submitting, listening, and confessing. At the end of the day, these actions are what we truly want our kids to have even more than winning. It's just hard to remember that. These principles apply to music, debate, art, and other activities too. In all this, remember our testimony as Christians is at stake! We have the opportunity not only to see our kids follow Jesus in every part of their lives but also to offer a testimony to the world.

Putting the Kingdom First

Jesus told us to "seek first his kingdom and his righteousness" as a general way to live (Matt. 6:33). What does this look like? Simply put, it means we focus more on training our children in the Lord than on the activity itself. Having fun is important, don't get us wrong, but when push comes to shove, we must choose the kingdom first. In the end, your child will enjoy the fruit of righteousness more than the gold medal. As you work this out in your own life, consider a few pieces of advice.

1. Make only limited exceptions. We should form our schedules around the kingdom and not the other way around. If all else fails, there are rare circumstances where you may elect to skip church for sports, music, or another activity, for example. Growing up, I (Chad) sometimes had to pick between church and travel hockey because championship games were often on Sundays, and my absence would put the whole team in jeopardy. Because my dad was a pastor, my parents couldn't easily skip church to come to my games. So we sometimes made an exception for those games, even though I had to skip church to do it.

2. Find a church service at a different time. Even when you make limited exceptions, though, try to find another worship service—even if not at your church. If your church offers different service times, simply find another time that works so you can still go to your important game. Or consider finding another church worship service on another night of the week. If nothing else, perhaps you can watch your church's online service at home or listen to the sermon audio together. If you simply can't find an alternative and the team's results would be in jeopardy, consider having a family worship time or devotion at home on the rare occasion.

> *Tell your child the why and not just the what about kingdom priorities.*

3. Talk about putting the kingdom first. Our final advice here is to tell your child the *why* and not just the *what* about kingdom priorities. If you're setting rules or boundaries in place that detract from their fun, explain to them what you're doing and why you're leading your family in that way. This is part of training your kids to put the kingdom first—making it clear at the heart level.

When We Prioritize the Kingdom

When we put the kingdom first, our kids will see how their activities should fit around the kingdom, not the other way around, as we mentioned. It's much easier, at that point, to disciple your kids to be humble when they play because you've shown them, off the playing field, what submitting to Jesus looks like. At that point, you not only tell them but also model to your children what putting God first means. When there are competing authorities, who gets priority—the team or Jesus? As disciple makers, parents personally need to wrestle through this dynamic and help kids see how they can work through it together, rather than ignore the tension.

Arranging your life around following Jesus rather than the NFL, for example, will yield a far greater result in your kids' lives. Although we'd like for our kids to make it to the big leagues—or even just the high school team!—few ever make a career of it. And if they do and you've discipled them, they will have learned to keep Christ at the center of their vocation. That's the story of many Christian leaders, such as Tim Tebow (NFL), Gabby Douglas (Olympic gymnast), Mike Fisher (NHL), Allyson Felix (Olympic runner), and Albert Pujols (MLB), among many more.

We're excited when we can prioritize God and still win. But what happens when we prioritize God and *don't win*? Do we give up prioritizing God at that point? That was the temptation I (Jim) had when I got mono during my senior year of college wrestling season, as I mentioned in Chapter 6. I was so angry at God because I had put Jesus first but had contracted an illness that eventually took me out of the sport. The closer I got to Jesus, the sicker I got. I didn't win the championship that year to become the four-time All-American I dreamed about. And ultimately, my dream to go to the Olympics died too.

At the time, I knew of stories like Eric Liddell, the famous Scottish Olympian who went to the Olympics, prioritized God, and won. This made me mad because I was building the youth group, but I didn't win at what I cared about the most at that time. While I don't think God gave me mono, he used my illness to help me prioritize his kingdom above sports. He allowed the dominos to fall in a direction that was different than I had thought I wanted or needed. That was a huge paradigm shift for me, and it changed my entire life—not just how I thought about sports. What did I learn? That winning is not everything. Following Jesus is, and the rest is just bonus.

All this goes to show that while we play and enjoy sports—or dance, play music, or participate on the debate team, whatever the activity—we should never let the activity take first place in our hearts. By your example as a parent, you show your kids and the world what following Jesus means, because the long-term spiritual journey is much more important than any short-term glory.

Bringing It Home for Parents

Here's what I (Jim) tell folks at our church: When you decide to put sports above church, you end up following your kids around. This shows them Jesus isn't first in your life. Instead, they see you putting them and their activities first. It becomes their ticket to having good friends or perhaps getting a college scholarship. If we spend all our time investing into their sports or music, they won't have time for youth group. Then their lives center around something other than God.

Even if they get that scholarship, they likely won't be prepared when they're exposed to teaching that contradicts what you believe about truth and about Jesus. They won't have the faith and relationships they need to help them weather the storm—because they didn't learn to prioritize the kingdom first. They didn't have time for spiritual friends because they were too busy aiming at earthly success—the success their parents prioritized. Essentially, if this happens, we hand our kids over to the world to be discipled by them. The result? A conversation at Christmastime that shocks you: your kids don't believe in truth, morals, or Jesus anymore.

If we prioritize the kingdom in every sphere, including play, though, we still have fun in the short term, but more importantly, we train our children to be faithful disciples of Jesus in the long term. Like Paul said, "Train yourself to be godly. For physical training is of some value, but godliness has value for all things, holding promise for both the present life and the life to come" (1 Tim. 4:7–8). We'd share this passage with any disciple, but we'll add a little bit for parents: train yourself *and your children to be godly* because the momentary sacrifices are worth it both now and in the life to come.

As we transition to the last of the Five Spheres of Discipleship, the spiritual realm, one point becomes clear: our battle is not against flesh and blood. It's more than that. We'll see how Sphere 5 brings together the other four spheres for the cosmic battle we're all engaged in as disciples. What role might humility play in this sphere? Let's find out.

Process the Acts 4 and Romans 13 Paradigm

We introduced in this sphere a way for disciples of Jesus to think biblically about what to do in the face of opposition. The Acts 4 and Romans 13 paradigm can be difficult to process, so we've created a short, one-time study to help you work through this paradigm in more detail. It's available for download at TheRevolutionaryDisciple. com/tools. Access "The Acts 4 and Romans 13 Paradigm" stand-alone study and take time to unpack these passages so you can better discern their meaning. Embrace the significance of this nuanced approach for yourself and your church, group, or ministry.

As a supplement, we've also created an additional stand-alone Bible study on Romans 14 about disputable matters, which we introduced at the end of Chapter 16. This resource is called "The Three Buckets Approach," which describes a framework for discerning how to determine if an issue is a salvation issue (Bucket 1), a fellowship issue (Bucket 2), or an individual issue (Bucket 3). Begin working through specific issues by placing them in each bucket. Download this study at TheRevolutionaryDisciple.com/tools.

Sphere 5

THE SPIRITUAL REALM

*Put on the full armor of God so that you can
take your stand against the devil's schemes.*
— Ephesians 6:11

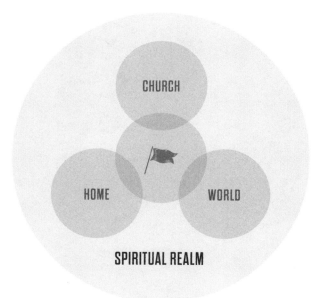

19

AUTHORITY IN ANOTHER DIMENSION

I n AD 53, the infamous seven sons of Sceva made a name for themselves performing extraordinary acts in the city of Ephesus.[1] Their father was a Jewish priest, and these brothers were casting out demons. But one day, they were totally unprepared for the results of a certain exorcism.

This story took place during Paul's third missionary journey while he lived in Ephesus. Paul was preaching and healing in the name of Jesus, and these seven brothers thought they could exorcize a demon with Jesus' powerful name. But they didn't know Jesus *the way Paul knew Jesus*. They wanted to use the power of Jesus without knowing the person of Jesus.

> *They wanted to use the power of Jesus without knowing the person of Jesus.*

They got a rude awakening when they tried to insert Jesus' name into their formula: "In *the name of Jesus*, whom Paul preaches, I command you to come out" (Acts 19:13). The evil spirit inside the demonized person called their bluff and said, "Jesus I know, and I know about Paul, but who are you?" (v. 15). Then the man literally jumped on all seven sons and physically beat them.

Luke tells us the seven brothers ran naked out of the house down the street, bleeding as they fled. These men walked into a spiritually-charged situation full of pride and walked away humiliated—from head to toe! It's sort of funny to us today, but we're sure they didn't laugh about it. Plus, the spiritual realm is serious business. They learned that Jesus is clearly not a name you can just *use* for personal gain. That didn't work for them, and it doesn't work for us today. The lesson? We must live with proper and orderly submission to the power of Jesus in the spiritual realm.

Just as in ancient Ephesus, people today also try to use the name of Jesus without a relationship with Jesus—also a result of pride. If we try to raise our family, be a good person at work, and do all these good things "in the name of Jesus" without a relationship of humility with Jesus, Satan will own us. The seven sons of Sceva tried to do a good thing—cast out a demon—but they did it without a relationship with Jesus. Instead, they operated in pride, and as a result, got the snot knocked out of them.

Different from the Other Spheres

Now it's a good thing we're on Jesus' side because we're all living through a fierce battle in the spiritual realm. We're fighting rulers and forces we cannot physically see. But they're real. We can't just waltz into spiritual battle, trusting in our own strength, and think, *We've got this!* Our strength is *in the Lord*, who calls us to right relationship with Jesus and with those in our local church body. As such, we need a working knowledge of how to fight the Evil One and his demons—together. If we don't, we can wind up flat on our faces like the Sceva brothers. That's why Paul calls us to "stand against the devil's schemes" (Eph. 6:11). It's not just in extreme circumstances we need humility in this sphere, though, it's all the time. As we'll see, this realm is not a separate, far-off place. It's all around us every day.

Sphere 5, the spiritual realm, is the last of the Five Spheres of Discipleship. It's distinct from the other four because it's not so much a different area of life as much as a different *dimension of life*. This sphere incorporates all of the others. After Paul tells us in Ephesians 1–5 of the other four spheres and what they should look like, he goes deeper into this dimension of discipleship in Ephesians 6.

The five spheres work together like this: As we learn to abide in Christ (Sphere 1), he puts us in the church to learn from others how to follow him (Sphere 2). Then, as we grow in Christ through community, we understand what family life at home looks like (Sphere 3). We take all of this into the world with us (Sphere 4). And behind the scenes is the spiritual realm with its own dynamics of authority and submission (Sphere 5). Hidden from our physical eyes, the spiritual realm affects our entire journey. We must navigate this dimension in humility like all the others. As we seek to do God's will and live according to his plan, the enemy comes against us, and we must embrace this reality. Our goal here is to help you see what it looks like to walk humbly with Jesus in "the heavenly realms" (Eph. 6:12). For starters, we simply need to acknowledge that spiritual authorities *actually exist*. Then we can start engaging them in battle.

Spiritual Forces in the Spiritual Realm

Paul describes our enemies as "spiritual forces," but he's not talking about some sort of cosmic energy like "the Force" from *Star Wars*. We're fighting actual forces that exist as spiritual personalities. We fight these forces in the "heavenly realms," as Paul calls it in Ephesians, and what we're calling the spiritual realm. We don't talk much like this today, so the terminology can be difficult to understand. Perhaps the simplest way to think of the spiritual realm is like this: it's not a place far off in the sky, *but the sphere in which we live every day*. So the spiritual realm, surprisingly enough, is the everyday realm around us we cannot see.

> *The spiritual realm is the everyday realm around us we cannot see.*

We call this a "realm" because it's more like a dimension in our reality than a place in the clouds. "Heavenly realms" in Ephesians is clearly not referring to heaven, as in the place we go when we die, because Paul's using it to describe the battle we fight here on earth— *in the invisible dimension of spiritual realities* (Eph. 6:10–18). Just because we can't see spiritual warfare doesn't mean it's not practical or even tangible! If we live without the spiritual realm in mind, then we do not live in light of reality. Many Christians struggle to live in the reality of spiritual authority.

Does fighting spiritual powers in this realm sound terrifying? We don't have to be afraid! Paul reminds us that the resurrected Christ is seated in the heavenly realms at God's "right hand . . . far above all rule and authority, power and dominion, and every title that can be given, not only in the present age but also in the one to come" (Eph. 1:20–21). In Christ, we have access to his power to fight against the devil's schemes because God has *"seated us with him* in the heavenly realms in Christ Jesus" (Eph. 2:6). As we've seen, Jesus lived humbly and died humbly. Now look at where he is—in the highest place of authority in the universe. Talk about a revolutionary way of life! Just like with Jesus, our exaltation takes place only after our humiliation. Now that we've laid the groundwork, let's look at Paul's vision for how this plays out in terms of beauty and strength.

> *Our exaltation takes place only after our humiliation.*

The Bride and the Warrior

I (Chad) was amazed to discover how Paul's vision for the body of Christ emerges when we look at Ephesians 4–6 as a whole. Paul shows how the people of God can move from infancy to infantry: We start as infants in the faith, "tossed back and forth by the waves" (Eph. 4:14). As we grow, we start looking more like full-grown spiritual parents, more like Jesus—the head of the church—"the fullness of him who fills everything in every way" (Eph. 1:23). At the climax, the body is built up "until we all attain to the unity of the faith and of the knowledge of the Son of God, *to mature manhood*, to the measure of *the stature of the fullness of Christ*, so that we may no longer be children" (Eph. 4:13–14, ESV). Notice the progression from infant to adult.

The end result of the process is "fullness," also known as maturity. As individuals we become more mature, but the church as a whole becomes more mature too. To use a sports analogy, the church grows as a team during a season. Good coaches take time to train a mature team. This means we not only grow taller or get older individually—spiritually speaking—but the church also becomes more formed, trained, and mature. The vision Paul casts in Ephesians 4 is realized in Ephesians 5—of a beautiful bride and a strong warrior.

Paul describes the church as a "radiant church, without stain or wrinkle or any other blemish, but holy and blameless" (Eph. 5:27). She's the bride of Christ. Paul's imagery connects with people on different levels. Those who want to look radiant connect with the image of the bride whom Christ makes holy and pure, and those who want to fight connect with the image of a warrior. But both work toward the same goal and the common vision of a strong, radiant, and unified church. As we become mature, we become both beautiful and strong. The final image in Ephesians is a warrior ready for battle.

Paul builds to the end of his letter to the Ephesians, where we see the cosmic battle between the fully armored body of Christ and Satan himself.

Take your stand against the devil's schemes. For our struggle is not against flesh and blood, but against the rulers, against the authorities, against the powers of this dark world and against the spiritual forces of evil in the heavenly realms. (Ephesians 6:11–12)

Now the church faces the enemy head-on through spiritual warfare. The image here is not of many warriors fighting together but all of us fighting together as one. It's called the body of Christ, and Christ himself is our head, our leader, and our authority. Because Christ is the head of the church, we must submit to his authority in spiritual warfare. That's how we win, as Scripture tells the rest of the story.

In the end, the revolutionary disciple is not just Jesus or us as individuals but all of us together. The revolutionary disciple is the mature body with Christ as our leader. We submit to Christ by fighting as one for what God wants. For us to take our stand and succeed in spiritual battle, we must first remember our identity. But we must also recognize that we have an enemy who seeks to destroy us: Satan and his minions. As a result, we are shrewd and humble in our walk with Christ. We're not just fighting sin; we're fighting a real enemy. Success in spiritual warfare, then, requires us to come humbly under Christ's authority—together as one. The rest of Paul's language captures the full impact of his battle imagery, which should encourage us to live faithfully today.

> *We submit to Christ by fighting as one for what God wants.*

Waging War as One

During the time Paul wrote Ephesians, ancient Roman warriors were known for their tight battleline formations. They had a chain of command to obey, and they fought as a group. They moved in battle as what's called a *testudo* (also known as a "tortoise formation"). This was a group of warriors who functioned as a single unit using their large rectangular shields to protect themselves as they walked together. Their formation helped them withstand the flaming arrows of their enemies. In this sense, they functioned as a single unit.

Their strategy required them to submit to one another and to their commander, which required each soldier to be humble. No one could break the pattern without jeopardizing the whole unit. Once they encountered the enemy, they shifted together from a defensive formation to full-on attack mode, where they sometimes fought in hand-to-hand combat.

We see these elements at play in Ephesians 6, where Paul employs this Roman army imagery to describe spiritual warfare for disciples of Christ. Paul describes our fight primarily in terms of hand-to-hand combat. We wrestle with spiritual forces in this realm. In fact, "wrestle" most accurately translates to the Greek word *pale*, which emphasizes the personal aspect of spiritual battle. Paul writes, "Our struggle (*pale*) is not against flesh and blood, but against the rulers, against the authorities, against the powers of this dark world and against the spiritual forces of evil in the heavenly realms" (Eph. 6:12). Our battle as disciples is up close and personal.

In Greek literature, *pale* described the most personal type of warfare at that time. A soldier's sword only helped him so far. Then he would have to fight his enemy face-to-face, wrestling them on the ground at times. Paul uses this term for on-the-ground wrestling to describe the battle we fight in the spiritual realm. If we don't recognize spiritual authorities and humbly abide by the rules of the engagement, we're bound to lose spiritual battles. We have to fight these forces together, not on our own. What does fighting this battle look like in our lives? Let's get real and bring this discussion down to earth.

20

VICTORY IN SPIRITUAL WARFARE

G o back with me to the story about when I (Jim) almost left Real Life Ministries, the church where I pastor today. I want you to see the spiritual battle at play in that scenario. In hindsight, I see how Satan worked to get me to leave the church. But I knew God wanted me to stay. I didn't feel peace about leaving, the Scriptures I was reading convicted me, and most of all, godly people around me challenged me with kindness and truth about what was really going on in my heart. The body of Christ stepped up to fight for me—*and with me.*

On all fronts, though, I was cornered. Satan had distanced me from Christ to the point I didn't want to pray or read the Word. I was angry that God had let this happen when I was not focused on abiding in Christ (Sphere 1). The enemy tried to divide our church leadership team (Sphere 2) and leveraged the existing challenges I had on the home front to attack me and my family. As I mentioned, my son had been dealing with a drug addiction prior to that time, which put an unbelievable—almost unbearable—strain on my marriage and home life (Sphere 3). Then I was tempted to leave my job in an ungodly way (Sphere 4). Do you see how Satan works all the angles in the spiritual realm to destroy us? He triggers our pride in various ways, which leads to isolation. Make no mistake: isolation is the breeding ground for spiritual defeat.

> *Isolation is the breeding ground for spiritual defeat.*

How Our Enemy Wages War

When we give in to pride, Satan gets a foothold and deftly moves into every area of life. It can start with a conflict, as in my story. Then, instead of working toward unity, we hide our anger and let Satan drive a wedge. First, the enemy starts to stifle our relationship with Christ. We begin seeing things from our fleshly perspective or from the world's ungodly point of view. Then we start building our lives on the sand instead of on the rock of Christ's Word. We think, *I'm my own authority. I don't need to rely on Christ for anything.* Yet Paul says, "We are all members of one body. 'In your anger do not sin': Do not let the sun go down while you are still angry, and do not give the devil a foothold" (Eph. 4:25–27). So we must fight pride by staying grounded with Christ.

When the battle goes south, Satan gains ground. If we don't think we need Christ to fight our battles, then we surely don't need the church. We start to think, *I'm fine on my own. I can't trust people anyway.* So we don't participate in church or in our discipleship group as often. Then Satan tries to take down our family by going after our marriage. At work, we're lured into developing ungodly habits. Before we know it, the devil has taken ground in every sphere.

Satan always tries to get us to believe that we can keep our lives compartmentalized. In the process, we believe the lie that we can allow him into just one sphere without it affecting the others. He'll settle for a small closet in one of the rooms in our spiritual house—a small, insignificant space. But he uses any space we give him to launch a full-scale attack on the whole house. He is a liar and never intended to remain in small spaces. Suddenly, we are lame ducks in his hand. He leverages our pride to destroy God's work in us. He's so predictable too: as soon as he lures us away from the pack, he devours us—his plan the whole time. And after he gets one of us, he tries to work through the whole group.

Our pride plays into Satan's agenda "to steal and kill and destroy" (John 10:10). He knows that if he goes for the root—our personal relationship with Christ—then he can sever us from our life source, Jesus, who came that we "may have life, and have it to the full" (v. 10). How do we resist the devil and experience life? By submitting humbly to Jesus in every area of our lives.

Now Is the Time to Get Moving!

If you'll remember, I (Jim) decided to stay at Real Life Ministries, even though I had a disagreement with the elders. I didn't want to stay—and definitely didn't *feel like staying*—but I stayed. As a result of God's work in our leadership, I saw God pour out his blessings on our church in the coming months and years in a truly amazing way. While I had given up on our church's progress on some big tasks at the time, God aided our progress in a completely different way.

Four years after I decided to stay at Real Life Ministries, the CEO of the Solomon Foundation came to our leadership team. He boldly challenged us, "You guys need to get moving. You've stepped back a bit from your willingness to have risky faith." He encouraged us to make big moves. Then another pastor came to speak at our church. While he was with us, we asked him to give our leadership team an outside perspective. After analyzing our situation, he said our desire to strengthen our disciples was apparent and good, but we may have become over-focused on internal church matters. He suggested we step out in "risky faith" to reach the lost again. He said almost the exact same words as the CEO of the foundation!

So after I finally submitted to the authority of the elders and we were a unified group—all submitting ultimately to the authority of Christ—a major change of heart happened. Our team responded with overwhelming agreement to these outside suggestions. All of the elders who had earlier wanted me to go slow now said, "Let's go!" Taking new ground as "one man" ended up being easy, just like the image of Roman soldiers walking side by side in Ephesians 6. By God's grace and power, we won the battle. And to think we almost missed it.

Our church ended up doing far more than what I had originally planned. In fact, this experience stretched me because it was so
much more than I had imagined. We experienced the unexpected
blessings of humility.

Blessings Poured Out

As a church, we ended up doing something none of us had previ-
ously discussed. Instead of building a bigger church building (my
original desire), we ended up building a massive sports complex the
whole community and surrounding region could use. Although I'm
a big sports guy (as you know by now), I hadn't thought about this
extreme way our church could contribute to the community. But
once it was on the table, I knew it was a great idea.

Today, we now have two artificial turf fields outside the sports
complex that allow us to host soccer, football, and other sporting
events. They're lighted fields, which is a big deal in North Idaho,
so our church can provide a year-round outside sports field for the
community. Additionally, we have a large steel structure with three
full-sized gyms inside it on our property, and we make it available
for leagues and school districts throughout the area. We also added
to our church building an all-new children's wing with an indoor
play area that draws young, unconnected families to our church. In
the first year alone after these expansions, we started thirty relational discipleship groups just to handle all the young families whom we
reached through the sports program.

Additionally, that first year we offered volleyball courts, wrestling mats, and a place to play for the sixty-eight kids who tried
out for secular school teams in our area but didn't make the team.
These kids now had something to do after school, and they were
in a church-run facility with Christian leaders in place. They were
able to see sports through God's eyes. These teams not only help us
reach those outside the walls of the church but they also give disciples with a passion for sports an opportunity to use their gifts in a
Christ-centered environment. The roster of every league is currently

filled to capacity. What's happening now and how God poured out his blessings on us is simply phenomenal. It's great we have so many people coming right now, no doubt, but for our team, we're experiencing something more important: *church unity.*

Once the COVID-19 pandemic hit, churches across the country and around the world became divided. Leaders were divided, church members left, and some churches even shut down completely. But because we had worked through building trust at a deeper level prior to that time, God enabled us to lead with great strength and unity during the pandemic. Because of the hard work wrought through reconciliation, we had become a unified team. So God actually grew our church during that time.

We had such an influx of new people that we had to start around a hundred new discipleship groups of various kinds and add staff members just to keep up. In fact, we ran out of space for our children in our new children's wing. Finally, we broke ground on a new campus not far from our main campus and are starting another one soon. So many decisions, connections, and impact! These are all great, but those on our leadership team know the greatest victory was the heart-level victory of our team's unity. That's really what led to this great expansion of our church. We weren't following our own plans but submitting, as best we could, to Jesus' headship over our church.

The Missing Piece to the Puzzle

What had gotten in my way before the blessings? I had operated in pride and not in Christlike humility. Once God helped me humble myself, he exalted himself in our team, the church. All of this occurred in the various spheres of discipleship, but ultimately the enemy had worked on me in the abiding sphere to destroy me in the spiritual realm. But I believe with all my heart that God spoke through the plurality of elders in the situation to save me and our church from ruin.

The hard part is submitting to others when we also have some degree of authority. We've heard many leaders say, "People should be under authority," but they exclude themselves from that and live like it's just "me and Jesus." But the Bible prescribes a plurality of elders because we all need their accountability and authority in our lives.

> *God fights our battles.*

It's why we're called to submit to God and to his delegated authorities wherever they are because God is in control and God fights our battles. We simply need to align ourselves with him and come under his mighty power, no matter what earthly positions we might hold.

I know myself well enough to say that while the battle for humility was won *in this case*, I struggle with my pride every day and often lose. I am so thankful for the constant and continual grace of God during that time and now. God gives me grace through my wife, my family, and my church—people who act as guardrails for me to tell me the truth when I have forgotten it. They remind me to choose to go lower.

Here's what I believe the Lord taught me through this: "Jim, if you move forward with broken relationships, it's going to fall apart from the inside out. Get the relationships right, humble yourself before me, and then we'll figure out the rest." Through this, I learned in a fresh way a lesson I had even taught others many times: it's not just about the task, it's also about the relationship. While I couldn't see the coming blessings at the time, I wouldn't have done it any other way now. I stayed at Real Life and fought together with my team simply because that's what walking together with Jesus in the spiritual realm requires. Our decision—the elders' and mine—to work it out thwarted the devil's schemes to divide our church.

We never graduate past humble submission to God's delegated authorities. Trust is the internal posture that results in this kind of submission. God uses our submission to transform us and those around us—but it happens in *his way* and in *his timing*. With this vision of the spiritual realm and a real-life example of what it looks like to fight in it, let's talk about what all this means for you.

21

LIVE TOGETHER, DIE ALONE

The TV series *Lost* first aired in 2004, chronicling the fictional
plane crash of Oceanic Flight 815 and its seventy survivors. The
survivors crash-landed on an island and had to fight to survive various enemies in a mysterious place far from civilization. The charac-
ters repeated a phrase throughout the episodes: "Live together, die
alone." If they stayed together, they would live; but if they tried to
survive alone, they would die.

That's a great line for the body of Christ. If we stay together in
spiritual battle, we live; but if we fight alone, we die. We're suscep-
tible to temptation anyway, but when we isolate ourselves, we weak-
en our defenses even more. Before we know it, our pride isolates us
in our battle with the evil forces in the spiritual realm. If we're not
aware of what's happening, it's sometimes too late to win the battle,
and we risk losing the war.

That's why Paul casts the vision in Ephesians 6 of *a fully armed
soldier*. In light of the battle we face, he calls us to "put on *the full
armor of God*, so that when the day of evil comes, you may be able
to stand your ground, and after you have done everything, to stand"
(Eph. 6:13). You might be used to thinking of Paul's description of
putting on the armor of God as an individual task. But Paul's not
writing to individuals; he's writing to the church. That's why the

church must fight *together*. As individual Christians and churches ask what's next for the church in the US and beyond, we propose a scriptural and timeless answer: walking humbly in every area of life—as one.

How to Navigate the Spiritual Realm

We emphasize unity in spiritual battle because the church needs this important and neglected message today. Why is unity so important? For starters, we fight against spiritual *forces* (plural). If we fight alone against an enemy of many, we act foolishly. Plus, Paul speaks to us as a group using plural language: "*You all* put on the full armor of God" (Eph. 6:13, AT). Yes, there's individual responsibility, but Paul writes to the church as a whole, encouraging and equipping us to fight together as one. This means we need each other to put on the armor and use it in battle. With this in mind, let us offer you some practical, boots-on-the-ground guidance for successfully navigating spiritual warfare with humility.

1. Go to God amid spiritual battle. Isolation threatens each of us, and we must learn to relate to God on a personal level, even when we don't feel like it. We must first go to God with our challenges instead of just trying to deal with them ourselves. It is the armor *of the Lord*, so we must go *to God* to get suited up. Pride keeps us alone and thinking, *I can take care of myself.* We must reject this and go to God in prayer and through his Word to get wisdom, guidance, and strength. When we seek God in these ways, instead of relying on our own wisdom, we walk in humility in the spiritual realm.

2. Rely on the church as you fight. We might successfully go to God as individuals, but pride again whispers, *You don't need to tell anybody else about your life, your struggles, or your sins. You've got Jesus and prayer—that's enough.* But the truth is Jesus gives us his church to fight spiritual battles *as the church*. Otherwise, Paul, a powerful individual in the kingdom, wouldn't need to write, "Pray also for me" (Eph. 6:19). Like Paul, we all need to rely on the church by asking for help through prayer and by receiving all sorts of encouragement. When we go to other people and let them fight with us and for us, we say, "I can't fight alone." That sort of confession requires humility, but it leads to victory.

3. *Fight for the church.* We know whom we fight *against* (the devil), but have you thought much about whom we fight *for* in spiritual warfare? Some people say we fight for God, which is true, but there's more here in Ephesians. People also say we fight through evangelism to win people to Christ, which is also true. But when you look at Ephesians 6 in context, these verses are not primarily about evangelism (if at all).

In Ephesians 6, Paul writes about *the church*, so we fight as the body of Christ *for the body of Christ.* Paul wasn't the first author of Scripture to talk about the armor of God. He borrowed the imagery from the prophet Isaiah. In Isaiah 59, we learn the armor of God receives its name because it's actually, you guessed it: *God's armor!* Let's look at the original context to see the full picture of Paul's words in Ephesians.

Fighting for the Church

In Isaiah 59, Isaiah describes a dire situation for the people of God in exile:

> The LORD looked and was displeased
> that there was no justice.
> He saw that there was no one,
> he was appalled that there was no one to intervene;
> so his own arm worked salvation for him,
> and his own righteousness sustained him.
> *He put on righteousness as his breastplate,*
> *and the helmet of salvation on his head;*
> *he put on the garments of vengeance*
> *and wrapped himself in zeal as in a cloak.* (Isaiah 59:15–17)

In this passage, God is the one who comes to the rescue.

We see the armor of God come into play here as God himself dresses for battle. God puts on righteousness as his breastplate and

the helmet of salvation on his head (Isa. 59:17). He puts on the garments of vengeance and wraps himself in zeal as in a cloak. Then
notice *for whom he's fighting:* Israel. This poetic description of the
Lord going to battle ends with God coming to Zion and fighting for
those who have repented (v. 20).

God is on a rescue mission, not a vigilante mission. Israel had
no hope against their enemies, so God himself stepped in to save
his people. This was prophetic, though, as he saved his people ultimately through his Son, Jesus. We know Paul uses Isaiah in subtle
ways throughout Ephesians, and this is another example.[2] Thus, Paul
describes the armor of God from this context in Isaiah. What a pro-
found connection! Paul says the church, as the body of Christ, takes
on the identity of God as a warrior. In humility, we accept this identity and fight with him.

When we do this, God equips us to fight with him for the restoration of the church. But we don't just fight with the church; we also
fight *for the church.* That's how we take ground.
Fighting alongside God reminds us how Jesus
invited us to learn from him *as we walk with
him* in Matthew 11:28–30.

> *God fights for his
> church through
> his church.*

Now we follow Jesus into battle as God
fights *for* his church *through* his church. When
we live into this high calling, we become the very hands, feet,
and voice of Jesus to redeem his church from the throes of Satan.
Remember, though, it takes humility to put on the armor, fight as
a team, and go where the Lord commands. And we must also heed
what Jesus said when we win in the spiritual realm: "Do not rejoice
that the spirits submit to you, but rejoice that your names are written
in heaven" (Luke 10:20). These words keep us grounded by remembering our salvation is the greatest victory.

Learning How to Fight in the Spiritual Realm

Now that we've got our bearings straight about the nature of our battle in the spiritual realm, how do we fight exactly?

1. Put on the full armor of God. We could look into the imagery of each piece of armor, but for our purposes here, let's look at the big picture and pick out a few high-level elements of the armor for spiritual warfare in general. We can leverage in battle the four tools we described early in this book: serving, submitting, listening, and confessing. We use these tools in the spiritual battlefield. In this way, our tools become *weapons* in the five spheres. But we can't put on our armor alone. God doesn't give every one of us a set of armor. We all share one set of armor and we put it on together—as one body!

Remember Paul's imagery from Ephesians 4:13 of the church as one man who has reached "mature manhood" (ESV)? And earlier Paul emphasized our oneness, saying, "There is one body and one Spirit—just as you were called to one hope when you were called— one Lord, one faith, one baptism" (Eph. 4:4–5). There's only one body of Christ, and we all wear the same set of armor. It's God's armor, not ours, so when we put on the armor of God, we actually suit up each part of the body of Christ with this gear. This understanding changes our perspective entirely from how we typically think of spiritual warfare.

Instead of fighting individual spiritual battles, we all help *each other* with the breastplate of righteousness to guard our hearts, we protect *each other* with the helmet of salvation, and we remind *each other* of the truth as we put it around our waist. These garments of battle are for the collective church, not just individuals who go to church.

2. Embrace the importance of fighting with words. One particular piece of armor stands out among the rest: the sword of the Spirit. Of all the armor, this is the only true weapon, and it's the key to winning our battles. Paul describes it as "the sword of the Spirit, which is the word of God" (Eph. 6:17). Perhaps you thought Paul was talking about the Bible here with the phrase "the word of God." But at the time of Paul's writing this letter, the Bible as we know it had not been codified, so Paul wasn't talking about the sixty-six books of the Bible. He wasn't even talking about the written words of the Old

Testament. We know this because of the specific word for "word" he uses here when he writes "the word of God."

The Greek language has two main words for "word": *logos* and *rhema*. While *logos* in the New Testament can carry a deep theological meaning—the organizing principle of the universe that Christ fulfills—*rhema* means something much more down to earth and practical. *Rhema* appears sixty-eight times in the New Testament, and it means *the spoken word of God.*[3] The spoken word includes the contents of the Bible, but it goes a step further here in Ephesians: it's when disciples speak the word of God out loud to one another. So taking up the sword of the Spirit means opening our mouths to speak God's word to help each other in battle. The spoken word is a strong theme throughout Ephesians, and it reaches its climax here in the armor of God discussion. So if we fight for the church with our words, what do we say?

> *Prayer is the native language of humility.*

3. Speak to God in prayer. Before we open our mouths to speak to one another, we must fight with our words through prayer. The first prayer we learn to speak as disciples is "I need help," which confesses our needs to God. Jesus then saves us because we've surrendered to his aid. Just like physical infants cry for help, newborn believers need a lot of spiritual help to grow up. But saying, "I need help," requires humility, as we've discussed. Prayer is the native language of humility because it says, "I can't do it on my own." Pride doesn't pray. But the humble disciple easily prays, "Lord, help me. I need you."

We pray for ourselves, and we intercede for the church. Paul instructs us, "Pray in the Spirit on all occasions with all kinds of prayers and requests" (Eph. 6:18). We pray about anything and everything because we need help in every sphere, and because everyone else in Christ needs help too: "Be alert and always keep on praying for all the saints" (6:18). We fight through prayer, but we also fight through speaking the truth to each other.

4. Speak truth to one another. Scattered throughout Paul's letter to the Ephesians, we find this theme of speaking truth.

- *"Speaking the truth* in love, we will in all things grow up into him who is the Head, that is, Christ" (4:15).
- "Each of you must put off falsehood and *speak truthfully* to his neighbor, for we are all members of one body" (4:25).
- "Be filled with the Spirit by *speaking to one another* psalms, hymns, and spiritual songs, singing and making music in your hearts to the Lord" (5:18–19, AT).

When we've carefully read Ephesians 1–5, this message about the sword of the Spirit in Ephesians 6 makes even more sense. By that point, we've got a strong understanding of what it means to "speak truth."

Our words can either build up or tear down. So Paul says, "Do not let any unwholesome talk come out of your mouths, but only what is helpful for building others up according to their needs" (4:29). And again, Paul warns, "Nor should there be obscenity, foolish talk or coarse joking . . . but rather thanksgiving" (5:4). Great power is in our words, and we must learn to build up the body by speaking truth to one another in the spiritual realm. *That's* how we fight and take ground in the hearts and lives of other disciples.

What does this look like practically? Knowing when someone in your small group is discouraged, and then speaking truth to them. Picking up the phone when the Holy Spirit prompts you to reach out to a friend so you can share a word from God's Word that's on your heart. Preaching, teaching, and encouraging truth in any and every form. Having family Bible studies. Singing songs together as God's people. Knowing and sharing Scripture from the heart to our brothers and sisters in Christ.

When Jesus fought the devil in the desert, what did he use? He didn't bring a scroll to the arid deserts of Judea. No, Jesus *spoke* the Word of God, which he knew by heart. That's how he fought, and that's how we're to fight too. By the power of the Spirit, we can effectively speak the Word of God to the people of God by the Spirit of God. That's how we fight for the body of Christ as the body of Christ.

To fight like this, we must be saturated in the Word personally and teach the Word corporately. Then together we can speak the Word to each other in the world and against the spiritual forces of evil that work inside the hearts and minds of fellow believers. Our words can literally usher in the power of God's Word to take ground for the kingdom, as we push back evil and God replaces it with good.

Do you know someone struggling with their faith? Speak truth to them. Do you know someone thinking of walking away from their marriage? Fight with words. Are the leaders of your church discouraged in their faithfulness to the gospel? Encourage them out loud. Your words can fight for souls. To do this, though, we must share our lives together—in community. We can't hide from each other if we're fighting as a team.

5. *Take off the spiritual mask and put on the helmet.* What we're learning here is not just to encourage others but also to allow others to encourage us. Here's a true story of someone who was not being open about their struggles, which represents where a lot of Christians are today.

I (Jim) met a visitor in our church foyer and decided to call him later that day. While he hadn't been coming to our church for long, he'd been there long enough for me to know who he was. So I called him that day and we connected. Soon after, I noticed that he had stopped coming to church, so I started calling him. For several weeks, he didn't answer. So I kept trying.

Finally, one day he picked up. I said, "How are you doing? I haven't seen you at church. Are you okay?"

"Oh, I'm fine. I've just been busy," he answered.

I'd heard this type of answer many times when someone's not doing well. So I said, "Something's going on with you. What is it?"

He said, "Okay, Jim, I'll just be honest with you. I can't put on my Christian face right now."

"What do you mean?" I asked.

"When I come to church, I can't put on my happy face, so I'm just staying home. I can't fake it."

"Why do you think you have to fake it at church? Shouldn't you want to come to church when you're struggling so you can be honest and get help? Who says you have to put on a face?"

"Well, that's not what I've been taught. I can't just go down there and pretend like everything's okay. So I won't go back to church until I can put the Christian face back on."

He had been wearing a spiritual mask, but he needed help putting on a helmet.

The problem with pride and wearing a spiritual mask can go deep. As we mentioned, the devil loves to keep us away from the church because he knows God's people can speak into our lives through the church. People believe lies that keep us quiet: *I can't show any weakness. I can't show that I'm struggling.* They think people will judge them, or they will be a burden to those who already have enough troubles. They think people will try to fix them—or worse, embarrass them. People ensnared by these devilish traps come to church only when they can appear happy or things are going well. But that doesn't allow others into their lives, and it doesn't allow the church to speak into their lives to fight for them. It's subtle, but their pride is keeping them away.

If Jesus, the Son of God, asked his disciples to pray with him in the midst of his great battle in the Garden of Gethsemane, then we can ask for help in our battles too. If Jesus could say in the midst of his struggle, "My soul is overwhelmed with sorrow to the point of death" (Matt. 26:38), then we mere human beings can admit our struggles too. Taking off our spiritual mask, being real, and showing our struggles or sadness in front of others takes humility. If we can't show our true self at church, then where can we show it? In Christ, we have the safest place on earth. It's called the church, and it's the only place where we can take off our spiritual mask and replace it with the helmet of salvation.

Our Call to Take Up Arms

In Paul's letter to the Ephesians, God calls us to take up arms and fight an important battle against the devil. This means we must first fight our internal enemy—pride. Only when we lay down and die to our pride can we truly take up the full armor of God in the body of Christ and effectively take ground in the spiritual realm. By now, you know that victory in the spiritual realm sphere relates to victory in every area of life. The revolutionary disciple surrenders their agenda for God's agenda and lives to serve. They listen to others and confess when they need help (and they help others too). This is walking humbly with Christ.

> *The revolutionary disciple surrenders their agenda for God's agenda.*

The spiritual realm sphere brings together all of the others. When we have a close relationship with Christ, we receive help from him (Sphere 1). Then we help others grow in Christ, which builds up the church (Sphere 2), impacts our home (Sphere 3), and helps us walk out our faith in the world (Sphere 4).

So put on the full armor of God, church! Take up the light and easy yoke of Christ and the sword of the Spirit. Let's engage in the battle *of the Lord* "so that when the day of evil comes, you may be able to stand your ground" (Eph. 6:13). And after we've done everything, we'll still be able to stand.

Sometimes all we can do is stand our ground, and that's okay. We don't always have to take ground or be the one giving of ourselves to others. And we don't always have to feel strong enough to fight. Sometimes all we can do is just stand. We're fighting together, so when we admit our weaknesses, others can fight with us and for us. It's okay to show weakness—to be humble and say, "I can't do it on my own." Because in Christ *we can*. In humility, we can grow up together in Christ and become mature. That's truly revolutionary—to have a whole group of people walking humbly and fighting for each other. Pride keeps us as spiritual babies tossed back and forth on the open waters, but God wants us to be filled up into "the whole measure of the fullness of Christ" living as a "radiant church" (Eph. 4:13; 5:27). God wants us to be strong and mature in him.

The choice is ours. If we learn from Jesus, we win, but if we don't learn how to navigate life in this sphere, we're dead in the water.

We'll remain divided, immature, and weak as disciples. Perhaps that's where you find yourself right now.

Perhaps you're battle-weary, having lost fight after fight. But you want to fight again. We've been there. So let us remind you that in Christ, there's hope. If we stand, God doesn't just give us the armor to fight; he fights for us and with us. Christ leads the way, fighting our battles, and we can look toward the final battle, when "out of his mouth comes a sharp sword" with which he will defeat all evil once and for all (Rev. 19:15).

We know that in the end God wins. If we remain faithful to following Jesus, we know we'll not only stand as brave warriors but also as the unified, powerful, and radiant bride of Christ. God, through the church, shines into the darkness of this world and brings forth a new dawn. And so we say with Paul from Ephesians 5:14 to those in Christ:

Wake up, O sleeper,
   rise from the dead,
and Christ will shine on you.

When we experience this type of revolution as the church, we reflect God's glory into the world. As we mentioned before, Paul says that "through the church, the manifold wisdom of God should be made known to the rulers and authorities in the heavenly realms" (Eph. 3:10). As we stand together as one church, united in Christ, we shine like a multi-faceted diamond in a dark world, showing off the great light of Christ to the powers that exist in the spiritual realm all around us. So we become strong and beautiful, and our beauty reflects God's glory. That is how we fight. That is how we win. That is how we walk humbly with Jesus in every area of life.

Fight with the Spoken Word

Now that you know about the importance of fighting for the body of Christ with words, it's time speak up! Engage with Scripture to understand better the power of the spoken word. Learn more about how Jesus used the spoken word to fight in the spiritual realm, and go deeper into Paul's use of the spoken word in spiritual battle. Use a study we created called "The Power of the Spoken Word," which is a one-time, stand-alone Bible study for individuals and groups to help you better understand how you can fight for the body of Christ with the spoken word. Download this study at TheRevolutionaryDisciple.com/tools.

We've also created a call-and-response group prayer that you can use to pray out loud with your church. It's called "Prayer of Mercy and Grace," which helps individuals and churches pray through the Lord's Prayer together in a personal way. Remember, prayer is one way we can fight with words. This tool comes with a reader's sheet, downloadable slides for your group, and a frameable PDF print with the words, "Lord, have mercy and give us grace." Download all this at TheRevolutionaryDisciple.com/tools.

Conclusion

A GLORIOUS ENDING

We've journeyed through the Five Spheres of Discipleship in this book, but as imperfect people, we are always learning how to walk in a way worthy of our calling in Christ. As we continue our journey, we may find ourselves going back and forth between spheres or up and down in our progress. Sometimes one step backward comes before two steps forward. Discipleship isn't a linear process. We can get stuck in certain seasons and even slide back a bit. But with God and other believers' help, we can get back and get moving again. As believers, we merely visit immaturity rather than live there. When the Lord whispers to us—or sometimes shouts— we are reminded of our calling, and off we go again, running hard toward the Lord.

What's Next?

Now it's time for you to take action as you continue learning to navigate the nuances of each sphere. As you learn how to live humbly on the level ground at the foot of the cross, we offer you the following signposts to reorient your continued journey with Christ. As you continue walking, remember these pieces of advice:

- Listen to God's voice, which convicts and encourages.
- Respond at the heart level by admitting your struggles.
- Repent of disobedience in any and every sphere, and then take action to humble yourself.
- Renew your commitment to Christ by totally surrendering every area of your life.
- Allow Jesus to architecturally redesign every part of your life according to his Word.
- Make the radical choice to allow your journey to impact others around you.

Like Josiah for his generation, we each have a choice to make for our generation. What is God calling you to do for your generation? What will you do with your slice of history? Remember that for every step downward along the path of humility, there's a corresponding step upward on the other side to glory. The cross always leads to the resurrection for disciples of Jesus.

> *The cross always leads to the resurrection.*

For His Glory

When I (Jim) decided to stay at Real Life Ministries, I didn't *feel* like staying. I stayed because it was the right thing to do. I knew I needed a revolution of the soul, and God was faithful to do it. Even now, I must allow him to do this daily as I pick up my cross and follow him. That's not easy for me. And I (Chad) didn't want to reconcile with my dad when I struggled with pride in our relationship, but God worked powerfully through our reconciliation to change my life.

For both of us, the unexpected blessings of obedience go to show that when we take the humble path of Jesus, God is faithful to us. When we choose to go low, God raises us high. We know Jesus reigns "in the heavenly realms, far above all rule and authority, power and dominion, and every title that can be given," but we must also remember that *we are seated with him in that high place of glory* in the spiritual realm (Eph. 1:20–21). And while we're now seated with him, we thank him for rescuing us from the depths of our depravity:

> God, who is rich in mercy, made us alive with Christ even when we were dead in transgressions. . . . And God raised us up with Christ and seated us with him in the heavenly realms in Christ Jesus, in order that in the coming ages he might show the incomparable riches of his grace, expressed in his kindness to us in Christ Jesus. (Ephesians 2:4–7)

The beauty of our journey with Christ is not just that we get to be exalted; it's that we get to be exalted *with Christ*. We've seen what it looks like to follow Jesus into the low places of humility in each sphere, but we're firmly seated with Jesus in the high places too, where we can enjoy the riches of his grace.

The same revolution that started with Christ and spread throughout the Roman Empire at the beginning of the first millennium is available to us today. If only we will humble ourselves, then God will hear us and heal our land. May your journey with Christ progress to the end as you walk in the humility of Christ—all for the glory of Christ.

When I (Chad) was younger, I would tell people what I wanted to do with my life. Half joking, I would say, "I want to start a revolution." Jim and I have both always wanted to change the world in a revolutionary way, but as we continue to get older, we realize that real change comes through small acts of faithfulness, which requires humility. We see this in Jesus, who focused his precious few years on earth discipling twelve men in a rural region of Galilee. He had a very short ministry, only three years, which the authorities eventually stomped out.

They took his body, but they couldn't squelch his message.

Jesus, the revolutionary, came to convert people, not coerce them into his kingdom, and that's a rare method of change in the world today. Yet the story of his gospel, the power of his message, and the radiance of his life reach us through the millennia, and he continues to convert hearts today.

While not everyone believes in Jesus, many know about him. Yet there's still work to do. The world needs change, the church needs change, *we all need change.* We need the humble heart of Jesus to continue changing us from the inside out, so that the world can increasingly experience the revolutionary nature of our King through the radiance of his bride. Christ in us is the hope of the world, so let's get moving and take ground together.

A NOTE FROM JIM

M y hope as you finish this book is that you are challenged to become a mature disciple of Jesus in every sphere of your life. At Real Life Ministries, where I pastor, we seek to make disciples in relational environments because we believe it's in relationship that we become relational people. Many years ago, our church started training other churches to do what we try to live out. We have trained thousands of church leaders in what we call "DiscipleShift 1." This is an experience rather than just a series of talks about relational discipleship. Leaders who have come for training and gone home to practice what they have learned have truly experienced change—not only in their lives as pastors and leaders but also in the trajectory of their churches.

We began coaching pastors from our church in North Idaho, and over time those who were in our coaching groups have become coaches of other pastors and their churches as well. As a result, we formed the Relational Discipleship Network, which is a network of hundreds of church leaders who have become practitioners of discipleship themselves. They are leading their churches to produce disciples who make disciples. In the end, I believe that spiritual maturity is not only our calling, but it also creates great friendships and support for those on the mission.

We would love to help you along your journey, through DiscipleShift 1 or through our network of churches. We have a great website for those interested in learning more about relational discipleship: rdn1.com. Through our training and network, you will discover a biblical way of making disciples and find friends who will coach and support you along the way. I hope to meet you at one of our training events.

— Jim Putman

Appendix

GROUP DISCUSSION QUESTIONS

We divided the questions below into the six major parts of this book, plus a few starting and ending questions. This structure helps groups who want to study the material of this book over a six-week period. If you want additional questions for a longer study—a handful of questions for each chapter—you can download them in PDF format at TheRevolutionaryDisciple.com/tools.

Starting Questions

1. How do you understand the role of humility in the life of a disciple of Jesus?
2. Is there a place for pride in the life of a disciple?

Chapters 1–4

1. According to Scripture, how was Jesus depicted as a "revolutionary"? See Mark 14:48 and Matthew 27:17–26.
2. What role did *the authority of Jesus* play in the Great Commission (Matt. 28:18–20)? Why does this matter for us today?
3. Pride can be easier to identify in others than in ourselves. How have you been convicted about pride in your life?

4. How does the story of King Herod's death in Acts 12:18–23 strike you?
5. What's your initial impression of this definition of a humble disciple: "A humble disciple knows who they are before God and chooses to go lower by serving, submitting, listening, and confessing"?
6. How have you seen humility modeled in others?
7. The four core practices of humility are serving, submitting, listening, and confessing. Of those, which is easiest for you to live out? Which is the hardest?
8. How might God be asking you to take a step toward humility? Are you willing to commit to that?

Sphere 1: Abiding in Christ

1. Read Matthew 11:28–30. What does it mean to take up "the yoke of Christ"? How is discipleship work? How is it restful?
2. Do you agree with the statement, "The revolutionary disciple accepts Jesus' way of life in every area of their life"? Why?
3. In what area of your life has pride affected your relationship with Christ? Have you allowed God to redeem that?
4. How have you prioritized working *for God* over abiding *with God*?
5. How does the story of the prodigal son from Luke 15:11–32 help you understand the role of the heart in humbly abiding with Christ? Read Luke 15:19 and 15:29 to see how each son's heart didn't always align with the father's heart.
6. Do you agree that in order to go effectively on mission for God we must humbly abide with him? Why? Read Isaiah 6:1–9 for reference.
7. Why is *listening* so important for walking humbly with Jesus?
8. Read Isaiah 66:2. What does it look like practically *to tremble* at God's Word?
9. What might God be asking you to surrender to him right now? Are you willing to commit to surrendering that?

Sphere 2: The Church Sphere

1. In Ephesians 5:23, Paul says, "Christ is the head of the church, his body, of which he is the Savior." Why is the reality of Christ's authority important for understanding humility in the church sphere?
2. How does our pride affect us in the church sphere?
3. How does Acts 2:42–47 help frame the essential practices of the early church?
4. Must a group have appointed elders in order to be a biblical church, or are elders optional? Why? See Titus 1:5–9 for reference (see also Acts 20:28 and Eph. 4:11).
5. What has been your experience with authority in the church? How might God be asking you to adjust your understanding of authority in light of the Scripture passages we've discussed thus far in this book? Are you willing to take action?
6. Why do we *need* the church as disciples of Jesus? Read 1 Corinthians 12:21 and Ephesians 4:11–12 for reference.
7. How have you struggled in the past with commitment to a particular church? Why was that difficult for you?
8. Are you committed to a specific church through membership? What benefit can you see in this kind of commitment?
9. Read Acts 20:28–31 and Hebrews 13:17. How do these passages help us understand God's heart about the authority of elders in the church?
10. What role can the church sphere play in other spheres, like the home and world spheres?

Sphere 3: The Home Sphere

1. Read Psalm 68:4–6. What is God's heart about the lonely? What might God be asking you to do in response to his heart?
2. How have you seen the church function as a family for the lonely?

3. Single parents, how can you take the next step toward allowing the church to help you? Married couples, how can you take action to welcome singles in your church? Are you willing to commit to that?
4. What does pride look like in the home sphere?
5. Read Genesis 3:16 with Ephesians 5:21–27. How does Paul's vision for the church here reverse the natural inclination of husbands and wives to control their spouse?
6. How might God be asking you to love your family as a whole better? Are you willing to commit to that?
7. How might God be asking you to love your spouse better? Are you willing to commit to that?
8. Read Luke 2:41–52. What is the significance for us that Jesus, the Son of God, obeyed his earthly parents?
9. Chapter 14 describes two forms of pride for parents: passive parenting and authoritarian parenting. Why is it hard for parents to reject these forms of pride in the home sphere?
10. How does a parent's confession to their kids reveal humility? Does it help or hurt their effectiveness as a parent?
11. How might God be asking you to grow in humility as a parent? Are you willing to commit to that?

Sphere 4: The World Sphere

1. Read Titus 3:1–2 and 1 Peter 2:13–14. How do these passages initially strike you?
2. What's a point of tension for you as we discuss church and the government?
3. Read Acts 4:19–20 and Romans 13:1–2. According to these passages, when exactly is it right to obey God over people?
4. Where does your primary loyalty lie?
5. Read Romans 14:1–4 (go to verse twenty-three if necessary). According to this passage, when should we keep our opinions to ourselves?

6. How might God be asking you to respond to the passages we've read so far in this sphere? Are you willing to take action?
7. Read Ephesians 6:7. Why do you think God cares about the state of our hearts at work?
8. How might God be calling you to humble yourself at work? Are you willing to commit to that?
9. Read Matthew 20:25–27. How does Jesus' heart about servant leadership inspire you?
10. How have you struggled with humility as you or your kids play?
11. Why is it important to allow God to transform us even in our hobbies, sports, and other areas of play?

Sphere 5: The Spiritual Realm

1. Read Ephesians 6:10–12. Why is it important for disciples of Jesus to be aware of authority in the spiritual realm?
2. What does pride look like in the spiritual realm? Humility?
3. The "spiritual realm," according to Paul in Ephesians, is not some faraway place but a dimension all around us. Why does this understanding matter?
4. How have you seen the enemy use isolation in spiritual warfare?
5. How have you seen God use church unity in spiritual warfare?
6. What does it mean to "be strong in the Lord and in his mighty power," as Paul says in Ephesians 6:10? Why is it important to know that *it's God's power*?
7. Read Isaiah 59:15–20. How does this help us understand spiritual warfare in Ephesians 6:10–18?
8. In Ephesians 6:17, Paul calls the sword of the Spirit "the word of God" and uses *rhema* (Greek), which means the "spoken word" of God (see how this word is also used in Matthew 4:4; John 6:63; and Acts 6:11–13). How is this nuance helpful in spiritual warfare?
9. How might God be asking you to engage in spiritual warfare right now? Are you willing to commit to that?

Ending Questions

1. What was the most encouraging part of this study?
2. What was the most challenging part?
3. What is God asking you to do next? What's stopping you from taking action?

NOTES

Chapters 1–4

1. The Torah is the first five books of our Bible today.

2. For example, the Peasants' War in the 1520s. See Martin Luther's *Against the Murderous, Thieving Hordes of Peasants* (1525) for Luther's response to this, which also included heavy-handed suppression of this rebellion. How exactly the Peasants' War related to Protestant theology is not clear. Surely some reformers did not intend physical rebellion, but people used Protestant theologians' ideas to support their rebellion toward the government for different reasons (economic, feudal, political). We are both Protestants, but for whatever the reasons, Protestants have historically sometimes acted in rebellion. That gives Protestantism a history of rebellion and stark independence. Rebellion is often rooted in pride, even on a national level and even with good intentions or clear reasoning.

3. Both of us live in the US, so we don't claim that our experience of Protestantism is true in every Western context. We do not intend to make absolute claims, just observations from our experiences. I (Jim) help train church leaders from all around the country and world, and I see people struggling through these pride issues almost everywhere I go. So while we're making statements about Protestantism in the US, we have a broad, even if still limited, perspective on this. Perhaps these issues go beyond our contexts, but we don't want to speak beyond what we know.

4. Bill Hull and Ben Sobels, *The Discipleship Gospel* (Nashville: HIM Publications, 2018), 24.

5. Learn more about the connection between the gospel, discipleship, and allegiance in Matthew W. Bates's book, *Gospel Allegiance* (Grand Rapids: Brazos Press, 2019).

6. John Dickson, *Humilitas: A Lost Key to Life, Love, and Leadership* (Grand Rapids: Zondervan, 2011), 99, 109.

7. C. S. Lewis, *Mere Christianity* (New York: HarperCollins, 1952), 130–131.

Sphere 1: Abiding in Christ

1. The mantle Elijah placed over Elisha signified a transfer of allegiance and covering. By accepting Elijah's mantle, Elisha accepted his authority.

2. The Greek verb here for "learn" is similar to the word "disciple" in Greek, so this is a true discipleship passage.

3. John C. Maxwell, *Developing the Leaders Around You* (Nashville: Thomas Nelson, 1995), 96–97.

4. Brandon Guindon, *Disciple-Making Culture* (Nashville: HIM Publications, 2020), 37.

5. R. T. France, *The Gospel of Matthew*, The New International Commentary on the New Testament (Grand Rapids: Eerdmans, 2007), Accordance electronic edition, 449.

6. See also 2 Corinthians 11:28 and Galatians 6:2 on this subject.

7. Dallas Willard, *The Spirit of the Disciplines* (New York: HarperCollins, 1988), 8.

8. See also 1 Peter 5:5; Proverbs 16:18; and Ezekiel 28:17.

9. Matthew W. Bates, *Gospel Allegiance: What Faith in Jesus Misses for Salvation in Christ* (Grand Rapids: Brazos Press, 2019), 114–115. Read his full treatment of how allegiance, faith, obedience, baptism, and repentance work together, including how the Holy Spirit empowers our good deeds, in Chapters 5 and 6.

10. Jesus submitted to God's righteous requirements through baptism (Matt. 3:14); to the local synagogue by preaching (Luke 4:16); to his parents by obeying them (Luke 2:51); to his father

by working as a carpenter (Mark 6:3; Matt. 13:54–55); to paying taxes to the Roman government (Matt. 17:24–27; 22:21); and to a trial under the Jews and crucifixion under Pontius Pilate (John 19:10).

11. Some people do totally abandon ship, though, such as Hymenaeus and Alexander. But even for those who have "shipwrecked their faith," there's still hope they will learn and be restored (1 Tim. 1:18–20).

12. The title of this book in German is simply *Nachfolge*, typically translated "discipleship." So it was not titled so much about *the cost* of discipleship, but just about what discipleship in general is like. We do not condone everything Bonhoeffer did during World War II, but his life as a whole was characterized by humility. See also Eric Metaxas, *Bonhoeffer: Pastor, Martyr, Prophet, Spy* (Nashville: Thomas Nelson, 2011).

Sphere 2: The Church Sphere

1. The early church focused on helping their widows and orphans, for example (see also Acts 6:1–6; James 1:27; 1 Cor. 16:1–3).

2. Watchman Nee points this out in *Spiritual Authority* (New York: Christian Fellowship Publishers, 1972), 92–93.

3. In Ephesians 4:1–13, the "gifts" are actually the people themselves (see v. 11) when you read the passage at face value, but we also know that in 1 Corinthians 12:28ff (among other places), every spiritual gift is from Christ.

4. With many cases of sexual abuse surfacing today as a result of church leaders' sin and malpractice, we will add an additional note here. Submitting to church leaders is the normal practice for all believers, but in cases of physical, emotional, or sexual abuse, believers should seek help and surface the abuse in an appropriate manner. They should also seek forgiveness, healing, and when appropriate, even reconciliation.

5. See N. T. Wright's book *After You Believe: Why Christian Character Matters* (New York: HarperOne, 2010), which touches on this topic, although from a slightly different angle. The title suggests

Wright's point that most people are familiar with the importance of conversion, but what happens after you believe?

6. See especially her lecture mentioned in the next note. This topic comes up also throughout her books *The Gospel Comes with a House Key* (Wheaton, IL: Crossway, 2018) and *The Secret Thoughts of an Unlikely Convert* (Pittsburgh: Crown & Covenant, 2012).

7. This comes from a lecture called "Immanuel Presents: Dr. Rosaria Butterfield - Peace in Sexual Identity," delivered at Immanuel Nashville in Nashville, Tennessee, on January 23, 2015, www.immanuelnashville.com/resources/multimedia/details?id=788970.

8. Butterfield, *Gospel Comes with a House Key*, 218.

9. For dating Paul's farewell to the Ephesian elders, see F. F. Bruce's commentary *The Book of Acts*, The New International Commentary on the New Testament (Grand Rapids: Eerdmans, 1988), Accordance electronic edition, 387.

10. 2 Samuel 5:4–5 tells us that David became king at thirty years old. Samuel anointed David when he was just a boy (1 Sam. 16:10–11; see also 1 Sam. 17:42).

11. Nee, *Spiritual Authority*, 82.

Sphere 3: The Home Sphere

1. This is from their American Community Survey (ACS). While father-only homes comprise only 8 percent of all US households, mother-only homes make up 25 percent of all homes in the US. These percentages are of total child population in married-couple, father-only, and mother-only households. Our summary of the data comes from the Annie E. Casey Foundation's Kids Count website, updated October 2018, accessed June 7, 2019, https://datacenter.kidscount.org/data/tables/105-child-population-by-household-type. Kids Count obtained their raw data from the US Census Bureau, accessed June 7, 2019, https://www.census.gov/programs-surveys/acs/news/data-releases/2017/release.html. See also American Fact Finder table B09005, factfinder2.census.gov.

2. A warning for single parents: While you do need help from people in the church, use discernment and wisdom about whom you allow into your child's life. Do background checks and ask several questions about a person before you allow them access to your kids. The Scriptures warn that the wolf will put on sheep's clothing to join the flock at times (Acts 20:29; John 10:12). Be very careful.

3. A warning to married couples here: Make sure you as a married person do not engage in a relationally deep way with someone of the opposite sex. Honor your spouse by protecting your marriage. In other words, men, don't visit the house of a single mom alone, even to help her with something she needs. Take someone else with you, such as your wife or another man from your group. That's just one example. Do ministry in twos; don't allow the devil to use something meant for good for evil.

4. C. S. Lewis, "The Sermon and the Lunch," *God in the Dock* (Grand Rapids: Eerdmans, 1970), 282–286.

5. Ibid., 282, 283.

6. Ibid., 286.

7. J. Oswald Sanders, *Spiritual Leadership: Principles of Excellence for Every Believer* (Chicago: Moody Press, 1994), 61.

8. For a scientific approach to the innate differences between women and men, see Jordan Peterson's *12 Rules for Life* (Toronto: Random House Canada, 2018). For example, see "Rule 11," starting on page 285. While we don't agree with Peterson about everything he writes (especially regarding the gospel), we believe he represents a fair-minded and data-driven approach from a clinical psychologist's perspective that demands more reckoning from the political and theological far left.

9. Stephen M. R. Covey with Rebecca R. Merrill, *The Speed of Trust: The One Thing That Changes Everything* (New York: Free Press, 2018), 1–2.

10. Gary Thomas, *Sacred Marriage: What If God Designed Marriage to Make Us Holy More Than to Make Us Happy?* (Grand Rapids: Zondervan, 2015), 9. We recommend this as one of our favorite books on the topic. Thomas writes how God's purpose in marriage

is not to make us happy but holy. Our spouses reveal our selfishness, and God uses those relationships like sandpaper to wood to expose our brokenness and make us holier.

11. Emerson Eggerichs, *Love & Respect* (Nashville: W Publishing Group, 2004), 42–44.

12. In his book, Eggerichs treats this topic in great detail with a much fuller explanation. See especially Chapter 5, starting on page 73.

13. In fact, the Greek word Luke uses here in Luke 2:51 for Jesus' submission is the same word Paul uses in Ephesians 5:21 for submission: "*Submit to* one another out of reverence for Christ." Also, Nazareth was topographically lower than Jerusalem, so even his physical journey downward represents for us his descent from his rightful place as the Son of God in God's temple to the humble region of Galilee.

14. For more on this, I (Chad), with my coauthors, Jason Houser and Bobby Harrington, included a whole chapter about discipline in *Dedicated: Training Your Children to Trust and Follow Jesus* (Grand Rapids: Zondervan, 2015), Chapter 8, "Dedicated to Discipline."

15. Be careful whom you ask advice from, even in the church. Some people don't know how to give good advice. They act like know-it-alls, but this is from pride, usually from young parents. As time goes by, parents realize they don't know what they think they know. So make sure to seek out parents you respect and who give sound counsel from a place of experience and not arrogance.

16. Houser, Harrington, and Harrington, *Dedicated*, 31–33.

Sphere 4: The World Sphere

1. A 2020 survey revealed that only 47 percent of adults in America belonged to a church, synagogue, or mosque, the first time in Gallup's eight decades of tracking this data. In 2000, that number was 70 percent. See Jeffrey M. Jones, "US Church Membership Falls Below Majority for First Time," *Gallup*, March 29, 2021, https://

news.gallup.com/poll/341963/church-membership-falls-below-majority-first-time.aspx.

2. As we mentioned, we condemn all forms of abuse, mistreatment, and neglect.

3. In Luke 3:14, soldiers asked John the Baptist what they should do in response to his teachings. John said they should not extort money or falsely accuse anyone and to be content with their pay. Then in Matthew 8:5, Jesus interacted with a Roman centurion to heal his servant. In these interactions neither John the Baptist nor Jesus told the soldiers to stop working as peacekeepers, which was a major part of their job.

4. A large number of Jews had been expelled from Rome by Emperor Claudius in the late AD 40s due to their rioting, but after Claudius's death in AD 54, Emperor Nero made it possible for Jews to return to Rome. Paul wrote Romans in the mid to late 50s, just after the expulsion decrees were rescinded. See N. T. Wright, *Romans* in The New Interpreter's Bible Commentary, vol. 10 (Nashville: Abingdon Press, 2002), 396, 406. So when Paul wrote Romans, the Roman church—made up of Gentiles and newly returned Jews (allegedly rebels)—was trying to figure out how they were to live under the Roman government. This plays into Paul's words in Romans 13 and elsewhere.

5. Obviously, we know from Scripture of special cases where God selected rulers like King Cyrus, for example, to act on his behalf, but this example and others must be understood in their context and not applied to all governmental rulers at all times.

6. Mark Ross, Professor of Systematic Theology at Erskine Theological Seminary, recounts this history: "The phrase occurs in a tract on Christian unity written (circa 1627) during the Thirty Years War (1618–1648), a bloody time in European history in which religious tensions played a significant role. The saying has found great favor among subsequent writers such as Richard Baxter, and has since been adopted as a motto by the Moravian Church of North America and the Evangelical Presbyterian Church." See his article "In Essentials Unity, in Non-Essentials Liberty, in All Things Charity," *Tabletalk*

(*Ligonier Ministries*), accessed March 31, 2021, https://www.ligonier.org/learn/articles/essentials-unity-non-essentials-liberty-all-things.

7. When Paul wrote these words, slaves made up about 10 percent, on average, of the population of a city throughout the Roman Empire, and as much as 30 percent in places like ancient Italy. James S. Jeffers provides this data about Greco-Roman slavery in *The Greco-Roman World of the New Testament Era: Exploring the Background of Early Christianity* (Downers Grove, Illinois: IVP Academic, 1999), 220–236. His helpful and detailed analysis of this time period shows us that ancient slavery in the Greco-Roman period was qualitatively different in many ways than slavery in US history and even many forms of slavery today. For a detailed treatment of this important topic about ancient slavery and the New Testament, see Chapter 11, "Slavery," in Jeffers's book mentioned above, especially pages 235–236. Ancient slaves sometimes shared harmonious relationships with their masters, and many slaves served wealthy masters, who offered them comfortable living, not to mention predictable food, clothing, and shelter. These slaves often had the ability to save enough money to buy their freedom. Plus, most slaves, at least in urban areas, were eventually set free, often by the age of thirty. Even after buying or finding their freedom, many slaves continued working for their masters as hired employees because their skills fit the bill and finding other work was sometimes hard.

8. Ibid., 227–228.

9. Chad Ellis tells this story in his book *Higher Power Selling* (self-pub., 2020), 76–82.

10. "Delaney," *30 for 30*, directed by Grant Curtis, aired August 19, 2015, on ESPN, accessed May 6, 2021, https://www.espn.com/30for30/film/_/page/delaney.

11. Ibid.

12. He contrasts that, rather playfully, with angels that "can fly because they can take themselves lightly." G. K. Chesterton, *Orthodoxy* (1908; repr., Nashville: HIM Publications, 2018), 152–153.

13. Gerard Manley Hopkins, "As Kingfishers Catch Fire," *Poetry Foundation*, accessed April 21, 2021, https://www.poetryfoundation. org/poems/44389/as-kingfishers-catch-fire.

Sphere 5: The Spiritual Realm

1. This story comes from Acts 19. With regard to the dating of this event, F. F. Bruce argues that Paul planned to leave Ephesus probably in AD 55, and this story happened while Paul spent approximately two and a half years in Ephesus. That's why this story likely occurred around AD 53. See *The Book of Acts* , The New International Commentary on the New Testament (Grand Rapids: Eerdmans, 2007), Accordance electronic edition, 381.

2. See also Isaiah 26:19 and 60:1–2 as well as Ephesians 5:14.

3. For *logos* see John 1:1, for example. For *rhema*, see examples in Matthew 4:4; John 6:63; and Acts 6:13.

ABOUT THE AUTHORS

JIM PUTMAN is the senior pastor of Real Life Ministries in Post Falls, Idaho. He holds degrees from Boise State University and Boise Bible College and is the author or coauthor of various discipleship books, including *Church Is a Team Sport*, *Real-Life Discipleship*, and *DiscipleShift*.

CHAD HARRINGTON is the owner of Harrington Interactive Media and a teaching deacon at Harpeth Christian Church in Franklin, Tennessee. He holds degrees from Ozark Christian College and Asbury Theological Seminary and is the author of *Your Spiritual Formation Plan* and a coauthor of *Dedicated*.